102 Great Dates FOR ANY BUDGET

"Happy Birthday"
Wilma

102 Great Dates

FOR ANY BUDGET

BY THE EDITORS OF SHARPMAN.COM®

Stewart, Tabori & Chang

New York

Published in 2005 by
Stewart, Tabori & Chang
115 West 18th Street
New York, NY 10011
www.abramsbooks.com

Canadian Distribution:
Canadian Manda Group
One Atlantic Avenue, Suite 105
Toronto, Ontario M6K 3E7
Canada

Library of Congress Cataloging-in-Publication Data

102 great dates for any budget / by the editors of SharpMan.com.
p. cm.
ISBN 1-58479-406-2
1. Dating (Social customs) I. Title: One hundred two great dates for any budget. II. Title: One hundred and two great dates for any budget. III. SharpMan.com.
HQ801.A5117 2005
646.7'7—dc22

2004025730

Edited by Jennifer Lang
Designed by Galen Smith
Production by Kim Tyner

The text of this book was composed in Futura.

Printed in China

10 9 8 7 6 5 4 3 2 1
First Printing

Stewart, Tabori & Chang is a subsidiary of

Contents

Chapter Three

Great Dates—Daytime

Chapter Four

Great Dates—Special Seasonal Dates

Appendix

Great Dates by Category

How to Use This Book

Just pick a date and go! Our great dates are organized into Evening, Daytime, and Special Seasonal Dates.

Each date description offers a variety of budget-sensitive means for planning the date, and includes a "Big Spender" version—for those all-out fantasy or special-occasion dates!

If you want to know more about what makes a great date work, take a look at our Intro section: you'll find useful tips on the elements of *any* great date (the "FACT"s), including information on first dates and *Advanced* Great Dating.

Need something in particular? Check out our key system:

Great for first dates

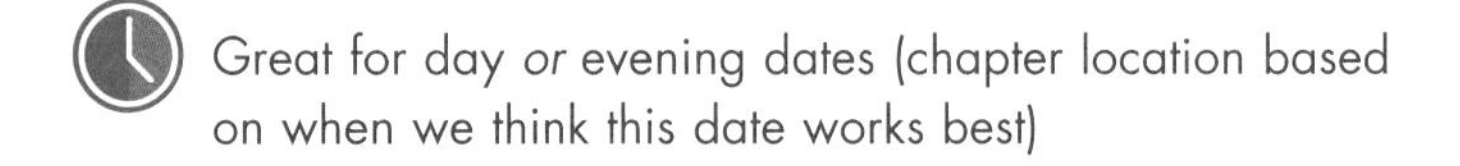
Great for day *or* evening dates (chapter location based on when we think this date works best)

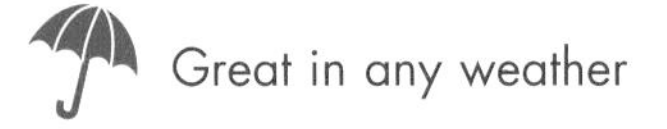
Great in any weather

Finally, don't miss the back of this guidebook for a complete listing of great dates arranged by category, including First Dates, Second Dates and Beyond, Dates for Day *or* Evening, and Dates for Any Weather.

Now, get to it!

Chapter One

What Makes a Great Date?

A great date is a well-planned date. For first dates, planning ensures that the person you're taking out has a good time, that you don't have to do all of the entertaining, and that costs are kept under control. The less you plan, the more your date will know it, the more pressure you'll feel to be entertaining, and the more you will spend in an attempt to compensate. Plan your date right, and all of your great date objectives will fall into place. And guys, she'll probably want to go out with you again, too. For couples, preplanning for a fun night out gives you both something to look forward to. In essence; your enjoyment of the date begins the moment you start planning.

How the Great Date Can Make a Big Difference

Whether it's your first date or your fiftieth, great dates can make a difference.

1st A guy's first date with a woman is likely to be the most important—the one where she decides, at least for now, if he's interesting enough to get to know better. In addition to other more obvious benefits, planning a great date will let her know that you've taken the time to ensure that she enjoys herself—and women *love* it when you've made an effort on their behalf. Plus, suggesting something fun makes it more likely that she'll accept the date in the first place, giving you a chance to work your charms.

Great dates are just as useful for those who've been dating a while and for married couples. A great day or evening out rekindles romance and can smooth over a recent relationship misstep. It reminds your partner why she said "yes" in the first place, and builds goodwill to ensure that she continues to do so.

Great Dates 101: The Elements of a Great Date

Building a great date is simple. Actually, it's a FACT: **F**ood, **A**ctivity, **C**onversation, and **T**hought. Get all four of these elements in, and you've got yourself a great date. Need more info? Consider the following:

Food

Must you feed your date? Yes. Sure, feeding a date can be pricey, but skipping this step risks throwing off the whole outing.

Why?

Simple: If your date coincides with a mealtime, your companion is likely to assume that there will be some food around *at some point.* With the evening wearing on and no food in sight, a hungry date becomes an unhappy date. Think of it this way: If your boss invites you over to his place on Friday night, it's not too far off to assume that the evening will include dinner *at some point.* If it's Super Bowl Sunday and your buddy tells you to come by, it's not unusual to assume that he's gonna have the game on *at some point.* Just as you expect the timing of certain invitations to include certain related activities, women assume that a date scheduled during a mealtime is bound to include *some* food. If you think about it, it's actually not that far of a jump.

This is why you shouldn't invite a woman out for "drinks" during dinnertime. If your budget can't handle dinner for two, plan an afternoon activity. Alternately, save money by planning a great date that calls for "grazing" rather than a sit-down meal (you'll find many in the Great Dates chapters of this guidebook).

The best reason for including food in your great date? Positive reinforcement. When you take a woman out for a good meal—even if it's just great burgers or inexpensive ethnic cuisine—you unconsciously signal that hanging out with you equals *sensory satisfaction*. Your date will associate delicious things with *you*. Not a bad badge of honor, if you ask us.

Activity

A great date should also include an activity *just* interesting enough to take some of the pressure off you. You're a date, not a clown, right? Don't set yourself up so that you have to do all of the work.

What kind of activity?

We've found that the best date activities—the real winners—are those that do more than entertain: They appeal to women's sensibilities on a *subconscious* level. Huh? That's right—some activities seem to *spell* romance. When you include one of these in your plans, it's as if half of the romance work is already done for you. Consider the following "DAPPER" great-date activity criteria:

DIFFERENT *Pick an activity that is a bit out of the ordinary. When a man surprises a woman with something she wasn't expecting, she automatically gives you romance points for coming up with something creative.*

ADVENTUROUS *Most lives are dull. Incorporating a sense of joint adventure into your plans—even if it's simply "discovering" a new neighborhood together—elevates the value of the evening.*

PLAYFUL *Being an adult can be a drag. Planning a date that allows the two of you to step away from your "grown-up" roles—have a little fun—earns points on the romance meter.*

PAMPERING *Consider planning a date around stuff you'd like to do* if you had the time. *Spending a leisurely day outdoors or simply working on a hobby can seem like decadent pampering—and highly romantic—to a busy person.*

ENTERTAINING *Good entertainment doesn't have to cost a lot of money. It also doesn't have to take a lot of time. But it does require careful planning. You will need to know what kinds of activities your date enjoys. Figure that out, and whatever you decide to do will be a winner.*

ROMANTIC *This one is gold. Consider capitalizing on the many years Hollywood has spent brainwashing us all. Plan your date around one of the "staple" Hollywood romance activities. Regardless of how cheesy they seem to you, women can't help but respond to them. You'd be surprised by how many guys overlook these obvious gems.*

All the great dates in this guidebook incorporate one or more of these romance principles. Watch for them.

$ Realize that a great date activity is not necessarily an expensive activity. In fact, we take the position that unless you are planning a special-occasion date (i.e., anniversary, birthday, etc.), you really shouldn't be spending that much money. *Money is not what dating is about.* For this reason, each of the great dates in this guidebook is presented in a modestly priced form ($0–$30) with a "Big Spender" version ($50 and above). You'll find our Big Spender suggestions ideal for all-out occasions and times when you'd like to pull out all the fantasy-date stops.

Conversation A great date also allows a couple to get to know each other. The activity you choose should not get in the way of good conversation. Of course, the *best* dates are those where the planned activity actually *promotes* easy conversation. Why is this so important? Because when your activity is entertaining *and* lends itself to conversation, your part becomes that much easier. You'll also find that certain activities are generally entertaining enough to compensate for lulls in the conversation. For this reason, all the great dates in this guidebook include activities that make great conversation starters.

Thought Finally, put some thought into what you plan. The more comfortable your date is with the activity, location, and her own wardrobe, the better time she'll have. Think about who your date is, what she would enjoy, and what will make her feel relaxed enough to have a good time.

Play to your audience. Pick an activity that she likes, a kind of food that *she* enjoys. Make it about her. Skip the stuff you like and she doesn't, along with those errands you were going to run while in the neighborhood. There's no sense in throwing away good date money if you're not going to get the maximum points out of it, right?

On that note, consider the planned location of your date: Will she be comfortable in a newly gentrified neighborhood or on a first date alone at your place? Some women wouldn't.

Not sure if she's up for a certain activity? Ask her a couple of questions about her preferences. Another good tip: Let her know what to expect. Give her a heads-up if she'll need a jacket, comfortable shoes, or a more casual outfit. As much planning as you put into the date, she's put more into her presentation. Don't let a simple failure to communicate ruin what could otherwise be a great date.

A Couple of Extra Tips for First Dates

For first dates, consider the following two great date strategy points:

TIMING When most women describe their ideal first date, the narrative usually ends with "and we talked all night." Sure, sometimes that works, but for the average first date "absence makes the heart grow fonder" is a much better strategy. For this reason, we do not recommend some of the longer outings in this guidebook for first dates. The idea is to give her a *taste* that leaves her wanting *more*. Sure, you're an amazing date—but hold back a little. Don't tell all the good stories and don't reveal all of your impressive résumé points. Plan a date that is entertaining and that lasts just long enough for her to decide to see you again. It's a great way to get a second date that leads to a third, fourth, and so on.

RIP

Another advantage to keeping the length of a first date short is the "too much" factor. Spending too much time together too soon can lead to chemistry death. You get sick of each other, destroying what could otherwise have led to a great second date and beyond. So remember, try to keep first dates on the short side.

COST This guidebook focuses on planning great dates that won't break the bank. A good time doesn't require a lot of money. If a woman likes a man, any activity that incorporates the FACT elements will thrill her, and if she doesn't like him, all the big-money dates in the world won't change that (and if they do, you're barking up the *wrong* tree, big guy). Of course, for special occasions with established sweethearts, try the Big Spender date ideas in each section!

$

This philosophy is particularly important for first dates. A first date shouldn't be about impressing a woman with a high-roller itinerary. It should be about giving each of you the opportunity to get to know the other. Is there a spark? Would you like to know her better? These questions are better answered in a relaxed setting where you have the opportunity to talk. High-end evenings, better saved for special-occasion dates, only serve to distract you from your examination. As for her, again, she either likes you or she doesn't; an expensive meal won't change her position. If it does, you may be dealing with an opportunist whom—no matter how good-looking—you shouldn't waste your time on.

But what about the competition? When guys take out women who get offers from many other guys, there's often a temptation to up the ante and plan a more expensive date. Forget it. First of all, you're setting an expensive precedent. Chances are you can't afford to make every date an all-out event. Second, your date may accept the offer because she'd like to try out that new restaurant, but she'll also happily accept another guy's invite for afternoon drinks and a nice walk. Wouldn't you rather be *that* guy? He's spending less *and* has the satisfaction of *knowing* that she's not out with him for the fancy eats. The bottom line? Women date whom they want. By taking women out on expensive dates early on—even if you can afford them—you risk being labeled as the guy she's dating for the pricey itineraries. Meanwhile, your competition is spending less and winning over the woman you want.

Finally, a bit of budget reasoning. Often you may be pursuing more than one woman at a time. Multiple pursuits (or "volume dating") require careful budgeting. But remember, low-cost dates do *not* have to be boring dates. Our many lower-cost great dates make volume dating more economically feasible.

Who Pays?

Every man must make this decision for himself. We take the position that since the guy generally extends the invitation, he's the host, and therefore he should pay. In the example about dinner at your boss's house, if he were to fork out dinner, you wouldn't expect him to hand you a bill at the end of the night, right? After all, the evening was *his* idea. *He's* the host. Similarly, when you ask a woman out, *you* are her host; the evening was *your* idea, and it kind of follows that you should "host" her.

Think about it another way: Paying is power. We're not talking about macho-guy control—that's a dating loser. On the other hand, the fact is that hosting someone gives you a sense of control over where you stand in the interaction. When you host, you're automatically the recipient of gratitude. This undercurrent is particularly helpful in the dating process. Why? Let's face it: It's bad enough that the concept of "courting" requires guys to put on a "good show." Call it a mating ritual or whatever, but the bottom line is that when guys take women out, they put on their smiling faces and their best manners—they're workin' it—because they're trying to win over their audience. The thing is, being the guy who "works it" (i.e., the Pleaser) is inherently a low-power position. On the other hand, when you insist on hosting the evening's activities, you shift a measure of power into your court. You're not some guy going "dutch," you're the Host, and you deserve her appreciation for your efforts. Get it?

This is another reason why all of our date suggestions offer economical alternatives. The idea being, if you are going to do all the paying, you gotta keep the budget realistic.

Advanced Great Dating

Once you've gotten the hang of great dating, consider incorporating some *advanced* great date elements. What are those? Advanced great dating allows you to spend the same amount of money while giving your date the *impression* that your evening is much longer and more elaborately (*and* creatively *and* romantically) planned. Advanced great dating also makes it easier to cut a bad date short without looking like, well, like you're cutting a bad date short.

Here are the basics: For a normal great date (and in all the great dates suggested in this guidebook), you generally plan two "legs" of the date. There's the activity leg and the food leg. The key to advanced great dating is splitting up these two main legs into smaller sublegs. For example, if your date is going well, consider breaking up the dinner leg into a main-course leg and then a coffee-and-dessert leg at another venue. Suddenly, you're not just taking her to dinner (coffee and dessert included), you're taking her to dinner *and then* you're also taking her to a cool place for dessert and coffee. The basic activity is the same, the cost is the same (sometimes *cheaper*), but you've gotten *twice* the mileage out of the same activity.

And advanced great dating doesn't end with dinner. Is she really great? Would you like to add another leg to the "activity" part of the date? Invite her for a walk in a picturesque area, perhaps to the place where your planned "activity" leg will begin. Not only do women consider walking *romantic* (weather permitting), the walk will save you money *and* extend the "value" of your date by adding another distinct activity. The trick is to always have a couple of staple "add-ons" to include if the date is going well.

And what about the bad dates? Sometimes it's pretty obvious that she's not for you—in fact, sometimes you end up locking horns before you even get to the restaurant. How do you bow out of a bad date without looking like a jerk? Advanced great dating takes care of that for you: When your date is composed of several distinct legs—each independent of the other—it's easy to give her the impression that one leg is all you planned and end the date by taking her home. You won't leave her with the impression that you're the world's most creative guy, but on the other hand, she won't feel that she's been dumped.

Got that down? Again, simply string together several activities to provide variation and allow you to make the date as long or as short as you like. To keep a date going, simply suggest another leg. To cut it short, cut off the remaining legs and take her home.

Now, for the great dates....

Chapter Two

Great Dates Evening

The Home-cooked Meal Date

The Date

Invite her over to your place for dinner à la you.

Why It's Great

Most people love a home-cooked meal, but women everywhere love when a guy takes the time to get his act together and make that homemade meal himself. We're talking *serious* points, guys. In fact, most women polled indicated that this was *the* most attractive thing a man could do for them.

You can plan to have the meal ready when she arrives, or prepare a few small items for snacking—while you cook and she watches. Easy conversation is pretty much a guarantee, as is your ability to control the cost of this date.

Big Spender Version

Add fresh flowers, tall white candles, or votive candles throughout your home. *Really* Big Spenders may wish to hire a formally dressed server to help with the food preparation between each course or arrange for a brief visit by an acoustic musician.

SharpNote

Check for food preferences and allergies prior to the date. Not ideal for the first date, since she may not feel comfortable hanging out at your place.

Required Gear

Ingredients required to prepare the meal. *Real* plates, forks, knives, glasses, and a clean bathroom.

The Indoor Picnic Date

The Date

A variation on the Home-cooked Meal Date (opposite), requiring you to lay out dinner at your place—with a twist.

Why It's Great

This great date may sound a little unusual, but it works like a charm, especially on a third or fourth date. As mentioned earlier, cooking a great meal for a woman is the surest way to impress the heck out of her. For an indoor picnic, just spread out a blanket and some pillows on your living-room floor and serve the meal there. The result is a dinner more unusual—and intimate—than simply sitting across the table from each other.

If you're planning a light snack, go for warm French bread with cheese (cut into a high-quality cheese like Brie—don't just slap down squares of Velveeta), strawberries, thinly sliced apples or grapes, and wine or champagne.

To cash in on the full potential of this great date, consider a complete meal. Since this *is* a picnic, focus on food that's easy to eat with your hands or without a knife. A successful menu may include shrimp cocktail, linguini with scallops in a rich clam sauce, and chocolate-dipped strawberries and champagne.

Big Spender Version

To make an even bigger impact, add props. Purchase a gingham picnic blanket, color-coordinated pillows, and a picnic basket. Your spread will look like it popped out of a catalogue, a movie, or *her dreams*.

SharpNote

Check for food preferences or allergies prior to the date. As with the Home-cooked Meal Date, some women may be uncomfortable hanging out at your place on a first date.

Required Gear

A blanket, pillows, real plates, forks, cloth napkins, glasses, and all the food you plan to serve. Add some low-volume music, a couple of candles or a fire, a clean bathroom, and you're ready to go.

The Psychic Friends Date

The Date

Book a psychic or tarot card reading for you and your date. Follow this up with dinner, a walk, and good conversation.

Why It's Great

Most people are intrigued by psychics, but few take the initiative to visit one on their own. By building a psychic reading into your evening plans, you instantly create a date that will be "different." The reading is bound to be a great conversation starter over dinner.

Plan for dinner at a restaurant that's walking distance or a short drive from where the psychic works.

Big Spender Version

The cost of psychic readings varies considerably. A street vendor may charge $5–$15 for a 20-minute reading, while some hour-long sessions can run several hundred dollars. Although a scarf-festooned place of business is fun, consider setting up a phone consult with a "psychic to the stars" in California or New York! To find a reputable celebrity psychic, do a bit of online research to determine which psychics have been featured on television shows. To contact them, call directory assistance or the television show producers, who regularly give out the contact information of their guests and experts.

SharpNote

A great first date.

We advise booking separate sessions for you and your date if you're on a first date or a date with a woman you don't know very well. To find a good psychic in your area, ask for referrals before resorting to the phone book.

Required Gear

An open mind.

The Wine Connoisseur Date

The Date

Taste and learn about various wines or liqueurs. Add lunch or dinner.

Why It's Great

Everyone wants to know more about wine, but most of us know nothing. Why not spend an evening learning about a subject you've been meaning to master? Many local wineries, restaurants, bars, wine clubs, and even local colleges hold regular classes. Tastings are generally geared toward those with a beginning-to-intermediate knowledge of wine, so there's no reason to be intimidated by "wine snobs." Many also include a discussion of how to match a wine with food, and are likely to include light appetizers—always a plus.

Big Spender Version

Looking for something more intimate? The wine stewards or sommeliers of most fine restaurants can arrange a private wine tasting that includes a selection of appetizers. In addition to "regular" wine, consider sampling dessert wines or after-dinner liqueurs. You're bound to learn something and leave your date wondering what else she can learn by hanging out with you.

SharpNote

To find a winery or wine-tasting class in your area, consult the classified sections of your local newspaper or search online. Alternatively, inquire at your favorite bar or restaurant.

Required Gear

No formal gear is required, but it might be a good idea to arrange for a ride home if you have too much to drink.

The Hometown Tour Date

The Date

Using a travel guide written for the town in which you live, take your date on a tour of the places most locals miss.

Why It's Great

Many guys feel pressure to take their dates to the newest, hottest place in town. After all, who wants to take her to the same places the last guy took her to? Forget all that. Consider taking your date to a few *old* places.

Buy a travel guide to the town where you live. What do outsiders travel to see there? Chances are that you've never been to most of the places described—even if you're a local. Plan an itinerary that includes a few of the places you'd like to go. The advantage to doing this at night is that there will be less traffic! Jot down the names of a few restaurants or cafés in the areas where you're headed.

When you pick up your date, show her the guide and your notes and ask her to add a few places that interest her. Cross out the sites that your date is familiar with and get going! Be sure to refer to the guide between stops. You'll be surprised by what you didn't know about your own town.

Big Spender Version

Call your local tourist board or chosen local spot to inquire about engaging the services of a local historian or expert who can meet you and your date to offer a short walking tour.

SharpNote

This is a fun first date. If your great date is planned for the evening, call ahead to ensure that the landmarks you're interested in aren't locked up or in neighborhoods best visited during the day.

Required Gear

Think comfort: Tourist clothing looks casual for a reason. A map is also a good idea, just in case. Throw a few drinks in the car or into a backpack if you're taking public transportation.

The Fair Date

The Date

Find a street fair, art fair, or carnival in your area. Spend the evening (or the day) riding, talking, and eating food that's bad for you.

Why It's Great

Sure, it sounds like the cheesiest date of all time, but there's something about this date—maybe the fact that it's the "staple" date in every teen-genre movie—that moves women to sigh.

Check out your local paper for a carnival, street fair, or similar event in your region. Even if the fair requires you to drive to the next town over, the car time will give you and your date a chance to talk.

Once there, be a fun date: Play the dumb games, win her a stuffed rabbit, go on as many rides as you can without hurling. Keep the snacks and drinks flowing. They're cheap compared to buying a nice dinner.

Big Spender Version

Visit the fair's management office to arrange a private fair experience for you and your date. Ride the Ferris wheel on a clear night with no one around. Add snacks and champagne in acrylic plastic flutes for extra Hollywood magic.

SharpNote

We recommend planning this date for evening in order to maximize the romance factor. A great first date, too.

Required Gear

Comfortable clothing and cash. (These events generally don't take plastic.)

The Classy Date

The Date

Take a class. Follow up with lunch or dinner.

Why It's Great

The experience of learning something together is a great conversation starter and an even better way to establish intimacy.

Got a first date? Sign up for a one-time class that she's interested in—the more interactive the better. Get to know your date while learning the fine art of clay throwing, screenplay writing, or knot tying.

For more ambitious guys courting steady girlfriends or wives, sign up for a six-week course on a subject you both enjoy. Add dinner. This will be a weekly date she'll look forward to.

Big Spender Version

Established couples looking for adventure may choose to take their class abroad. Many touring companies offer one-week to one-month classes in regional cooking, wine, architecture, art, and even cinema. Often these firms are owned by native English speakers living abroad. For example, Scale Reale (www.scalereale.org) is a "school" in Rome run by Harvard University–educated architect Tom Rankin. The service offers walking tours and hands-on courses in all aspects of local Italian culture.

In addition to consulting travel guides, contact the American or Canadian chamber of commerce or consulate/embassy in the city where you would like to study. Try to cross-reference your choice with the Better Business Bureau's online service (www.bbb.org).

SharpNote

To find a class in your area, check out your local university. Community colleges and local high schools often offer the best deals for your money—as little as $10 per class.

Required Gear

See course requirements. Mostly, you just need a good attitude.

The Classy Date—With Food

The Date

Take a cooking class and fill up on what you've learned.

Why It's Great

This variation of the Classy Date (page 35) has a plus: It includes food. Yup, you get to go through the whole bit about "learning" with your date, and then you get to eat for the same price. Not a bad deal.

The nice part is that, these days, you can choose your class according to your appetite. Are you a dessert fan? You can take an entire evening class devoted to chocolate. In the mood for sushi? In Los Angeles, the California Sushi Academy has the class for you.

Big Spender Version

Contact your favorite local restaurant. Periodically, chefs will offer cooking classes for small groups. You may even convince him or her to make it a group of two.

SharpNote

Consult the White Pages for cooking schools in your area. As with the Classy Date, local universities, community colleges, and high schools offer cooking classes—one-time or ongoing, some as low in cost as $10 per person.

Required Gear

See course requirements. Comfortable shoes and aprons are always a good idea.

The Big Dance Date

The Date

Take a dance lesson for two. Follow it up with lunch or dinner and a drink at a bar where you can practice your new moves.

Why It's Great

Ever wonder why women dig those old Technicolor movies? Part of it is the *dancing*. Most women love the idea of hitting the dance floor and actually looking *good*. Be the man to make that happen for her. Sure, you may not be able to dance a step *now*, but after a lesson you'll be the Fred Astaire to her Ginger Rogers. Very high on the romance meter.

Most dance schools can teach a wide variety of styles. If you don't know what type of dancing you'd like to learn, make an appointment and decide when you get there. On the other hand, if you're interested in salsa dancing, many clubs that have salsa nights offer "early bird" lessons before the dancing begins. In some cases the lessons are free with a two-drink minimum.

Formal dance classes can be kind of pricey, so shop around. Private classes will cost you the most, but group classes are less. After dinner, head over to a club where you can trip over each other and have a great time.

Big Spender Version

Paying the premium for a private dance lesson is one thing, but arranging a private *rooftop* practice session, complete with lighting, music, and champagne, is quite another. Many hotels with roof gardens close these areas in the evening. Arrange to "rent" a space in exchange for the champagne purchase. In many cases, these areas are ideal for dancing in that they are clean and prewired for sound, and you can easily arrange for food and drinks. Most important, they are large enough to allow you and your partner to practice all of your moves.

SharpNote

Since learning to dance can be frustrating, this may not be an ideal first date.

Required Gear

Comfortable dress shoes work for most dance lessons. Advise your date to avoid high heels for the first lesson.

The Taste Test Date

The Date

Tour a series of local eateries in search of the perfect version of one type of food or beverage.

Why It's Great

This date has three things going for it: variety, easy conversation, and a sense of a joint mission. Combine all three, and you have everything you need for a great date that makes an impression.

Here's how it works: Do you have a favorite food? Does she? Is there a type of food that your town or region is known for? Consider conducting your own "taste test" by hopping from one food source to another, each of you making notes or discussing the attributes of the version at hand.

If you haven't discussed this plan with your date prior to picking her up, bring along a local restaurant guide such as the Zagat Survey or a listing of recommended eateries from your newspaper. Pick the type of food you'll be reviewing, locate three to five restaurants serving this fare, and head out for your first stop. After each tasting, you and your date should independently rate the food for several factors (i.e., taste, consistency, presentation) and then discuss why the rating was given. Unless you two are busy chomping or in a post-food coma, there won't be a silent moment all evening.

Big Spender Version

Ever wonder what the difference is between sevruga and beluga caviar? Set up a taste test of this or any other extravagant food that is considered a price-point delicacy. Other choices include truffles (the fungus ferreted out by specially trained "truffle pigs"), foie gras, abalone, shark's fin, or a fine cut of steak.

SharpNote

When ordering, think "less is more." After all, wine tasters don't sample an entire bottle at each stop; too much spoils the appetite of the taster.

Required Gear

Bring along any guides or reviews you find, two small notebooks, and pens for your ratings. For last-minute restaurant picks, consider bringing a mobile phone to ensure that each of your choices is available prior to your arrival.

The Photo Date

The Date

Spend the evening on a photo safari for two.

Why It's Great

It's pretty much guaranteed she hasn't been on a date like this before. It's different, fun, and you'll have plenty to talk about.

Pick up two cameras, one for you and one for your date. Your mission—should you choose to accept it—is for you and your date to cruise town, snapping away at things and people who interest you. Alternatively, you can choose a theme to work with.

Drop off your film at a one-hour photo development place (several major drugstore chains provide 24-hour one-hour developing) and head off to dinner. Pick up your photos and check out your "exhibition" over coffee and dessert.

Big Spender Version

Use two digital cameras instead—you can print your own work or download your memory cards at a photo-lab kiosk. The lab will "doctor" your work to reduce red-eye, fix unflattering facial shine, or slim down, um, body parts. For a final touch, pick up two small photo albums—one for her and one for you—for showcasing your best work.

SharpNote

A great first date or hundredth date that includes souvenirs.

Required Gear

Two cameras. Haven't got one or more? Disposable cameras work just as well, but spring for the ones with a flash, particularly if you're planning an evening date. Bring along extra film or extra disposable cameras.

The Amusement Park Date

The Date

Spend the evening (or day) enjoying rides and junk food at a regional amusement or theme park.

Why It's Great

This one's another magic-movie-moment date. Sure, the rides are fun and often romantic, but better still, this date lets you piggyback off years of Hollywood programming that have convinced most women that amusement-park dates equal romance.

Besides, a woman who will agree to go skydiving with you is rare, but most enjoy thrill rides at amusement parks. Combine this with plenty of time outside, tons of walking and conversation, and the occasional close encounter on a "scary" ride, and you've got bona fide date success.

Be sure to be generous with the snack food and refreshments.

Big Spender Version

Many amusement parks now offer a pass that allows you to skip the lines for an additional fee—*well* worth a Big Spender's dollar if lines aren't your thing. Another way to step up this date? Souvenirs, and lots of them. Pick up every item on her girlhood wish list—all the stuff that her parents used to say they didn't "have room for in the car."

SharpNote

The amusement park is not a bad first-date idea, but between the cost of admission and the overpriced food, even the cheap version of this date may be a little pricey for your first time out with a woman. Consider saving this for special occasions. Also realize that there are a few women out there who hate roller coasters, experience motion sickness, or simply think theme parks are downright dumb. Know your date before hitting the highway.

To find an amusement park in your area, contact your local tourist board. Some amusement park companies, such as Six Flags, claim to have a park within "one day's drive" from any family living in the contiguous United States (www.sixflags.com).

Required Gear

Comfortable clothes and walking shoes are a must.

The Draw Your Luck Date

The Date

Rather than choosing one activity for your date, choose and plan three.

Why It's Great

Any date that begins in an unpredictable way is a good date. Everyone loves surprises and adventure; this date combines both. Pick three dates from our list or yours. Write a short description of each on a small piece of paper, fold, and place in a hat. Your date chooses. We suggest that each outing require the same type of gear and dress, so that you and your date are prepared regardless of the activity she draws. Of course, you can always show her the dates she *didn't* choose ("What's behind door number one?") and change plans if she prefers. Play to your audience.

Big Spender Version

The good thing about this date is that the amount of money you spend is dependent upon the types of dates you put in the bag. For instance, if you toss in "Go see tonight's NBA game," it will cost more than "Go bowling." Generate date ideas depending on how much you want to spend. When your date picks a slip out of the bag, she will never know what the other options are until you tell her.

SharpNote

Works just as well for a first date as for a weekly date with a longtime companion.

Required Gear

For the opening act, you'll need paper and a pen to write out the date descriptions and a hat or other container from which your date will draw. Be sure to bring along any other gear required by the three date options you choose. Again, we advise choosing dates that require similar gear.

The Taking Off for Vegas Date

The Date

Pick up your date and head out of town for the evening. Don't forget "road food" for the full effect.

Why It's Great

There's nothing quite like picking up an unsuspecting dinner date and announcing, "Honey, we're goin' to Vegas!" Of course, not all budgets and regions allow for this spontaneity. Fortunately, almost every town has some type of entertainment center within a few hours' drive. OK, maybe it isn't Vegas, but any town with more going on than your immediate area can make for an exciting—and surprising—evening, rife with good conversation and entertainment.

Don't forget the essence of all last-minute road trips: junk food for the car and plenty of stops at roadside attractions, like the World's Largest Ball of Twine.

Big Spender Version

Call or e-mail your date telling her to wait outside her home for you (or a hired car and driver). Tell her she needs to be dressed and ready, with a suitcase containing [X] number of day outfits and [X] number of evening outfits for [type of] weather. Greet her outside her home or meet the hired car at the airport, bearing flowers and two tickets to your Sin City of choice.

SharpNote

Unless you already know your date well, this one is not an ideal first date.

Required Gear

Call ahead to check out what's going on at your destination. Look into restaurants and shows to make sure that your version of "Vegas" hasn't closed for remodeling. Also, be sure to get good directions to your various destinations, and bring along a good map, just in case.

The "Local Culcha" Date

The Date

Check out some local theater or other events. Add dinner.

Why It's Great

Most guys are so focused on "fancy" entertainment (i.e., THE Theater, THE Symphony) that they often forget about all the great—and less expensive—local theater and music offered in their town or region. Check them out. Most towns have interesting local theater projects, tons of great bands, and even classical music offerings that rival the pros (well, sort of). All of these offer an outstanding opportunity to show your date how tuned in you are to cool happenings right around you. That's right, you're *cultured*. A great impression and a fun date. Throw in some dinner—preferably at yet another local gem—and you've got a great date.

Big Spender Version

Established couples—especially married ones—hardly ever seem to work local culture into their schedules. Between grocery store runs, carpool, and cleaning up around the house, who thinks about "culcha," anyway? Why not bring the "culcha" to you? Call your local university music department or peruse the Yellow Pages for a music-booking agent (like those who book corporate events) and hire a formally dressed string quartet to visit your gal while she does stuff around the house or visits with friends—it will be a day she'll never forget. Follow this up with a night out on the town for maximum points.

SharpNote

A variation on this date includes a play or other performance at her old alma mater. That is, assuming her experience there was a good one.

Required Gear

You'll need a local paper to figure out what's going on. Then check out a restaurant guide to add a cool eatery, preferably within walking distance of your entertainment venue.

The Animal Romance Date

The Date

Spend the evening at a local zoo. Include a picnic dinner.

Why It's Great

Sure, zoos are for kids—during the day. Many zoos also offer special evening hours that allow visitors to check out numerous nocturnal species at a time when the zoo is much less crowded. Additionally, many zoos feature jazz or other music series during the summer months. This provides an ideal opportunity to take your date somewhere different and enjoy some great music, a nice walk, and easy conversation. Since most zoo concession stands offer only marginal fare, consider packing a romantic picnic dinner, complete with wine and a picnic blanket. Just spread out on a grassy area or bench by your favorite exhibit and enjoy the view. Remember to focus on feeding your date, not the animals.

Big Spender Version

Arrange for a private tour of the zoo. If your date has a particular interest in a species of nondangerous game, it may also be possible to arrange an up-close-and-personal visit into this habitat. Most zoos are woefully underfunded and depend on private contributions to build new habitats and maintain existing ones. Often zoo benefactors—even modest ones—receive additional benefits such as private zoo viewing and tours by zoologists. Call the fund-raising department of your local zoo and inquire as to the contribution level required for this opportunity. It is likely that the contribution amount will be equal to or greater than the cost of a private walking tour anywhere else. Alternatively, call the zoology department of your local university and inquire about hiring a professor or graduate student for this purpose, as many zoology departments have privileges at local zoos.

SharpNote

This date works well for first dates, but will backfire if your date thinks zoos are cruel to animals.

Required Gear

To find out what your local zoo offers, call or visit the zoo online. Don't forget the picnic and a heads up to your date about wearing good walking shoes.

The Top of the World Date

The Date

Spend the evening checking out the local sights—from far above—by visiting various aerial viewing points around your city. Add dinner.

Why It's Great

It's cool when an outing provides a fresh perspective on something familiar. Why not check out your own city from a different angle? Prior to your date, locate a number of buildings, scenic hilltops, and other locations that provide excellent views of your city. Take your date from one spot to the next and attempt to locate the same home, school, or other structure from every viewing point. Add plenty of snacks along the way and top it all off with dinner at a restaurant with an amazing vista.

Big Spender Version

For the ultimate in evening city viewing, consider hiring a helicopter for an hour's ride around your town. Check with smaller airports in your area for helicopter rental services. In smaller towns, many news and weather reporting agencies periodically hire out their helicopters and pilots to offset operating costs. Arrange to have the pilot drop you near your dinner destination, and take a taxi, car service, or limo back to your car.

SharpNote

Call ahead to arrange access to the top floors of private buildings. Consider packing a picnic and creating your own scenic eatery at her favorite of the spots you visit.

Required Gear

Comfortable walking shoes are a must. Depending on the weather, you may also want to bring along a couple of jackets for the outside viewing points. Consider packing lemonade or hot chocolate, depending on the season.

The Auction Date

The Date

Attend an auction or check out an auction preview. Add lunch or dinner.

Why It's Great

Everyone loves "stuff." Whether buying or just looking, there's something really satisfying about perusing quirky art, collectibles, and jewelry. Combine this love of stuff with the excitement of an auction, and you've got a winning date combination. After all, it's hard *not* to get into the action at an auction; they're designed to draw you in and make you feel like you're having a good time. Plus, with so many types of auctions to choose from, you're bound to find one that interests your date.

No chance to get in on the action? Consider attending the "auction preview," an evening prior to the actual auction when the sale items are on display, along with wine and cheese for those who attend. Spring for an auction catalogue (usually about $10)—a great memento of your "highbrow" afternoon or evening. Follow the auction or preview with dinner.

Big Spender Version

Get in on the auction! Prior to your outing, ask your date what she collects or is otherwise interested in. Pick her up and hand her a catalogue featuring the items up for auction that night. Over dinner or drinks, invite her to circle any lots on her wish list. Then head to the auction and bid!

SharpNote

A great third date and beyond. Less appropriate for first dates, as there may be some discomfort around the issue of money and bidding.

Find out about the auction scene in your area by checking out the classified section of your local newspaper. Churches, schools, and other organizations also often hold charitable auctions. Attending one of these is a great way to show your date that you are interested in philanthropy.

Required Gear

"Nice date" attire is advised for the auction scene.

The Karaoke Date

The Date

Find a karaoke bar in your area and sing your hearts out. Follow with a Japanese lunch or dinner.

Why It's Great

Singing at the top of your lungs isn't just for Japanese executives anymore. This date idea will *really* help you and your date open up and let loose. If it is just the two of you and you are on a first date, stick to the general area of the bar.

Big Spender Version

Many karaoke joints offer private rooms (called *notabung* suites) that allow you to invite a few friends along and enjoy private food and beverage service.

Alternatively, rent or purchase your own karaoke machine and invite some of your date's friends over to your place for a night of singing. With your own machine, you can sing all night long. Include lots of snacks to keep the party going.

SharpNote

A fun first date. Inviting friends is suitable for third dates and beyond. Inquire as to your date's comfort with this idea prior to planning your evening; some people know they can't sing, and a forced singalong could spell D-I-S-A-S-T-E-R.

Required Gear

Vocal cords and confidence!

The Riding by the Light of the Moon Date

The Date

Steal away for a romantic horseback ride during a full moon.

Why It's Great

Forget dinner and a movie. This is one outing that your date is sure to remember; plus, you'll score extra points by saving your date that dreaded, proverbial question: What do I wear? For this date, jeans, boots, and a comfortable shirt or sweater are a must.

Call around to local stables to find one that offers moonlit horseback rides, or query local riding clubs and instructors. Afterward, stop by your local coffee shop and enjoy lattes as you celebrate your new careers as urban cowboys.

Big Spender Version

Extend this date by booking a stay at a nearby dude ranch, where you and your date can play "cowboy" and "cowgirl" for an entire weekend. Dress the part in denim, hats, and boots. When you're not riding, slip away for some quiet time for two.

SharpNote

A dude ranch stay may not be appropriate for first dates.

Required Gear

A full moon and clothing suitable for horseback riding.

The Foreign Lands Date

The Date

Rent a video from another country and get takeout to match.

Why It's Great

Renting a kung fu movie and getting Chinese takeout is relatively inexpensive and a great way to do "dinner and a movie" with a twist. Alternatively, try a Bollywood movie and takeout Indian food. Throw in an Indian hip-hop CD as your dinner mood music. This date is fun, relaxing, and perfect for rainy nights in.

Big Spender Version

For fun evenings out or lazy weekend afternoons, take in your foreign film at the local art house and visit a restaurant that serves the cuisine from the country where the movie takes place.

SharpNote

Some people aren't into movies with subtitles, so you may want to opt for a film from an English-speaking country or rent a DVD that has the option of watching the English-dubbed version. The at-home version of this date is not appropriate for first-time get-togethers.

Required Gear

A foreign movie and the phone numbers and menus of several ethnic takeout restaurants.

The Give Me S'mores Date

The Date

Load up some firewood and head to the hills for an evening of campfire stories and s'mores treats.

Why It's Great

As if a woodsy night sky and a fire weren't romantic enough. You're throwing in s'mores? Be still, our beating hearts. Actually, the process of making these childhood treats prevents this date from getting too "out in the woods" serious. Plus, building a fire showcases your manly "roughing it" skills.

Can't build a fire to save your life? Cheat it by picking up fire starters called "fat sticks," which are designed to be placed below your pile of wood. Just light a match and—voilà!—you're in the s'mores business.

For the s'mores you'll need:

Graham crackers (regular or chocolate-flavored)
Large marshmallows
Solid chocolate candy bars
Wire hangers or barbeque forks for marshmallow roasting

Big Spender Version

Take advantage of that fire and atmosphere with a romantic campfire dinner prior to your s'mores dessert. Consider cooking your meal in a Dutch oven or simply packing meat and veggies in aluminum foil to be warmed up by the campfire flames. Bring along some nice dishes and plastic picnic wineglasses for a touch of romance.

SharpNote

A date in the dark, dark woods may not be appropriate for a first-time outing. Also, check to see if fires are permitted before you pick your spot.

Required Gear

Firewood, matches, s'mores ingredients, wire hangers or barbeque forks, and refreshments.

The Game Night Date

The Date

Play some of your favorite games: old standbys like Scrabble, Candy Land, and Monopoly, or new brain busters like Cranium and Scattergories.

Why It's Great

A little friendly competition never hurt anyone. Taking turns playing each other's favorite games allows you to learn more about each other between rolls of the dice—and all in a relaxed setting. Make it a full night in with delicious takeout.

Big Spender Version

Spice it up by inviting your date into a toy store. Peruse the board-game aisles and choose one neither of you has played. Then pick up a takeout dinner and learn how to play the new game together. Or, after a round or two of Scrabble, grab something to eat and head to your local arcade to play some of your old video favorites.

SharpNote

A great date with a woman who's bringing her kids, or a fun date for a rainy afternoon.

Required Gear

Games, snacks, and lots of quarters if you decide to go to the arcade.

The High School Rewind Date

The Date

Regardless of whether you had an awesome prom night or you'd rather leave that bad memory behind, re-create your prom night with our high school rewind date—minus the teenage anxiety, bad haircuts, acne breakouts, and curfews!

Why It's Great

Always wanted to take your dream girl to the prom? Here's your chance. Don your best suit and take your date out for a night on the town. Begin the evening with a corsage (on a budget? Clip some greenery and flowers from a nearby bush, add safety pin). Be sure to pull out all the stops: Take the obligatory preprom photos, walk arm-in-arm, open the car door, and make reservations at a swanky restaurant. Can't afford a five-star eatery? Eat your meal at a more modest restaurant and have dessert at the pricey one.

Afterward, wrap up the evening with a private dance at your place—complete with white holiday lights strung from the ceiling, party favors on the table, and soft music in the background.

No interest in reliving your prom? How about attending one of your high school's football games? Nothing compares to the excitement of a high-school game. Plus the *other* entertainment—the actual high school students—should give you and your date plenty to laugh and talk about. Make a few trips to the concession stand to feel like a big spender at your old school.

Big Spender Version

High school rewind is a great way to help your date erase any old prom memories that were less than ideal. Follow some of the same guidelines listed above, but instead of driving yourselves, rent a limo for the evening—complete with champagne and fruit. Reserve the corner table at a five-star restaurant; order appetizers, drinks, and dessert.

Follow dinner with a stay at one of the top hotels in your town. Remember how classmates used to pool their money for a hotel suite after the dance? No need to pool now. Bring along a CD of music from your high-school era for private slow dancing in your luxury suite. The next morning, send flowers with a note thanking your date for the most memorable prom night of your life.

For the high-school football alternative to this date, plan a private tailgate party for two (that's code for high-school football-themed picnic, very romantic).

SharpNote

This date is a great follow-up to the Scrapbooking Date (page 152). The hotel suite addition to the Big Spender version of this date is not appropriate for first dates.

Required Gear

Corsage, music, and information about your date's high school.

The Mixin' It Up Date

The Date

Make a day or evening of compiling a tape or CD with your date's favorite songs. Then pop it in for an afternoon drive or dinner.

Why It's Great

Nearly everyone is passionate about one type of music or another. Who hasn't had that moment of reminiscing when a certain song comes on? Why not add this special flavor to your date?

This date encourages conversation about the songs you're collecting (as well as the musicians and events of that time in your life)—and it memorializes the time you spend making the tape or CD together. Your date will think of you every time she hears these songs again. The CD is a great date souvenir for both of you.

To plan this outing, ask your date to bring along favorite CDs. Break out the old CD/tape deck boom box or prepare your CD burner, and buy a few blanks. After the tape is recorded or your CD is burned, listen to it as you relax over a meal.

Big Spender Version

To add another dimension to this date, purchase tickets to the concert of one of your date's favorite performers and surprise her with the tickets at dinner, while the performer's songs are playing from the mix-tape or CD.

SharpNote

Perfect for those first-date "get to know you" conversations. But note that some women may not be comfortable spending time in your home on the first date.

Required Gear

A blank tape or CD and a stereo with dubbing capabilities, or computer with CD burner.

The Mexican Night Date

The Date

Make authentic Mexican food or order in and let the margaritas flow. Make sure your music sets the theme.

Why It's Great

This date lets you flex your cooking muscles and have a great time doing it. Choose your menu from a Mexican cookbook and do all your shopping before the date—don't forget the margarita mix. The best way to make this date fun is by setting the mood with Latin music CDs and by having a margarita ready for your date as soon as she walks in. Next, get cooking. Allow your date to help you prepare the food, and munch on chips and salsa as you cook. Even if the food doesn't turn out exactly as planned, after a few margaritas, neither of you will care. The key is to keep the spicy theme going. Suggest salsa dancing after dinner to make the night red-hot.

Big Spender Version

If you're not a fan of cooking, have your meal catered. Order in from an authentic Mexican restaurant in your area, and the only time you'll spend in the kitchen is mixing up more margaritas. For added fun, hire a mariachi or salsa band for a few hours and make room for dancing!

SharpNote

Because of the "bad breath" factor of Mexican food, this may only be suitable for third dates and beyond. Check with your date to make sure she has no food allergies. Note that some women may not be comfortable spending time in your home on a first date.

Required Gear

Ingredients and a blender for the margaritas, limes and salt for the glass rims, Mexican food fixings and, um, *breath mints*....

The Movie Marathon Date

The Date

Find out your date's favorite type of movie and rent three from that genre. Don't forget the popcorn. Invite friends and set up chairs for a movie-theater feel.

Why It's Great

Not only is this a cheap and simple date, but it makes your special someone feel, well, special. It's a date that is all about her, and will be more memorable than any fancy dinner. To pick your flicks, casually inquire about your date's favorite type of movie or favorite actor. Make a trip to your local video store, and rent two or three movies that reflect this preference. Better still, rent movies your date will realize that *you* would never pick but are willing to endure for her. For example, pick up the *Die Hard* trilogy for your Bruce Willis fan. Or, *Dirty Dancing* might be more your date's taste but not high on your list. She will appreciate your thoughtfulness.

Don't forget all the movie-theater fixings!

Big Spender Version

To step up this date, rent a theater screening room for the night. Lead your date to believe you're seeing a movie, and usher her into the empty theater that has been reserved just for the two of you.

SharpNote

Although this date is fun when other friends and couples join in, it's a good idea to hold off on inviting others until after your third date.

Required Gear

Video or DVD and various candies and popcorn for an authentic movie-theater feel.

The Swingin' Date

The Date

Pick out swing-dance costumes from a vintage store (or your parents' attic) and take lessons, or try out your moves at a swing-dancing club.

Why It's Great

When Mikey shed his shyness and twirled Lorraine around the dance floor in *Swingers*, a twenties dance craze was revived in the nineties. For swing-dancing newcomers, lessons are a must. Schedule a session at a local dance studio so that you and your date can get off on the right foot. As a surprise, stop by a local vintage or thrift shop and pick out some swing-dance-friendly dresses—it's much more amusing to learn the steps when you look the part. Once you and your date have learned the basics, head to a club and try out your moves on the dance floor.

Big Spender Version

Although professionals make it look easy, swing dancing is an art form perfected with practice. If your date is a long-term partner, spring for a series of swing-dance lessons for the two of you.

SharpNote

Great for first or fortieth dates. Make sure to schedule your lessons in advance. Check the newspaper for dance-lesson listings.

Required Gear

Pop in the *Swingers* soundtrack to get in the mood. Swing costumes can be assembled from thrift shops or vintage stores. Comfortable dancing shoes are a must.

The Book Lovers' Date

The Date

Go to a bookstore or library, pick out favorite novels or poetry books, and read passages to each other.

Why It's Great

For people who enjoy reading, this date is a great way to share a part of themselves. And it is absolutely free! If you choose to read at a bookstore, make sure to scout locations ahead of time. Pick a store that offers comfy overstuffed couches, so that you and your date can feel at home. Better still, many bookstores now feature cafés where you can purchase coffee and a few snacks if you don't plan on eating later. For those with a personal collection of books or books borrowed from the library, pack a blanket and a picnic, and park both under a tree for the ultimate book-lover's afternoon.

Does your date have a favorite author? In most cases authors will tour bookstores in major cities to read from their new work. Why not make a date of it? Surprise your date with plans to hear her favorite author read at a local bookstore, then treat her to a copy of the work!

Big Spender Version

Why read passages to each other at the bookstore when you can purchase the books and create the ultimate romantic evening in your home? Find out your date's favorite books ahead of time, pick them up, and set up a romantic picnic surrounded by candles in your living room. See the Indoor Picnic Date (page 27) for more information. Make cushions and pillows plentiful, keep the wine flowing, and create a meal that corresponds with the mood or setting of one of your date's favorite books. It will be a night she'll never forget.

SharpNote

This date is only suited to people who love books. Be sure to confirm this prior to planning your date.

Required Gear

If you plan this date at a location other than a bookstore or library, bring your personal collection of favorite books and ask your date to do the same.

The Open Mic Date

The Date

Take a date out to an open-mic night—where you or both you and your date will perform.

Why It's Great

"Open mic" is exactly what it sounds like. Audience members at a comedy club or bar have the chance to get up onstage and perform comedy or play an instrument. Most entertainment venues have one or two nights devoted to open-mic participants. Call a local comedy club or music venue for dates and open-mic protocol.

As for an open-mic date, it's an activity that really gets the heart pumping. You and your date's open-mic performance might be a crowd pleaser or have the audience yawning. Whatever the outcome, it will be a memorable joint experience.

Big Spender Version

If you and your date are apprehensive about going onstage with an untested routine, invite her to join you in a stand-up comedy course. To find a comedy or improvisation class, call a local comedy club. You and your date will have a chance to plan and practice your material under the guidance of a professional comedian, who will fine-tune your timing and delivery.

SharpNote

Definitely not for the faint of heart, as public speaking is a great fear for many. As such, inquire as to whether your date is up for this activity prior to planning.

Required Gear

Stage clothing, special props, and confidence.

The Star Studded Date

The Date

Sweep your date away from city lights to enjoy a night of stargazing.

Why It's Great

Stargazing has always spelled romance. Everything about it is conducive to intimacy, from huddling together for warmth to leaning back and staring at the heavens to pointing out the constellations.

Prior to your date, research the constellations. The Internet can provide an accurate view of the heavens in your area. You'll find that a powerful flashlight or green laser can be used as a pointing device.

Choose your stargazing spot carefully. The higher up you go and the farther away you are from city lights, the more stars you and your date are likely to see.

Be sure to bring along a thermos full of coffee or hot cocoa and food that's convenient to handle in the dark. For bonus points, consider stargazing-related foods such as Mars bars, Milky Ways, croissants, cheeses (think moon), and SunChips.

Big Spender Version

Many universities have astronomy departments with access to an observatory. Call ahead to arrange for a stargazing session or lecture on astronomy for a fee. Alternatively, consider renting a tripod telescope and purchasing a star chart for a better view of the sky on your own time. Small handheld telescopes are a lower-cost alternative.

SharpNote

If you plan to stargaze in a remote area, this date may not be appropriate for first outings.

Required Gear

Warm clothing, reclining chairs, star charts, and a backpack full of hot chocolate and treats.

The Somethin's Fishy Date

The Date

Enjoy a traditional fish fry with your date.

Why It's Great

You don't have to wait for Friday night for a traditional fish fry. It's a blast any night of the week, and is especially fun if you cook the fish at home, where you can set the mood and music of the evening. Even if you're not the greatest cook, it's hard to mess up good old fish and chips. Buy fresh fillets of a good white fish, dip in salted flour, heat up a deep fat fryer or several inches of cooking oil in a heavy pan, and you're all set to fry! Although you may have your own, consider this Indian-inspired recipe:

4 large fish fillets, each cleaned and cut into 2 or 3 pieces
Salt to taste
1 teaspoon turmeric
1 tablespoon lemon juice
4 teaspoons red chili powder
1 tablespoon garlic paste
1 tablespoon ginger paste
1 teaspoon ground coriander
1 tablespoon tamarind pulp or kokum peels pulp
Oil to deep fry
4 tablespoons slightly coarse rice powder
Onion slices and lemon wedges, for garnish (optional)

1. Wash the fish thoroughly and add salt, turmeric, and lemon juice. Set aside for 10 minutes.

2. Stir together the chili powder, garlic, ginger, coriander, and tamarind and set fish in this mixture to marinate. Refrigerate for about an hour.

3. Heat the oil. Roll the pieces of fish in rice powder, one by one, and deep-fry in batches on medium heat until crisp.

4. Garnish with the onion slices and lemon wedges.

Big Spender Version

Go all-out for the whole "English pub" theme: Serve ale or cider, rent a Monty Python flick, dim the lights, and settle down to enjoy the laughs and terrific grub. There's no better way to get to know your date.

SharpNote

Fish can be fried whole. Clean the insides, wash well, and make deep incisions or gashes on both sides, then proceed as above. Your fishmonger can do this for you if you prefer.

To make this recipe low-fat, the marinated fish can be pan-fried or grilled with a minimum amount of oil instead.

Not ideal for a first date, since she may not feel comfortable hanging out at your place.

Required Gear

Ingredients, cookware, table setting, and (for fish and chips), french fries and newspaper. Don't forget to clean your bathroom.

The Progressive Dining Date

The Date

Play epicureans for the day by visiting as many local eateries as you can. Make it a progressive dining experience, where you eat appetizers at one restaurant, dinner at another, and then dessert and coffee at a third.

Why It's Great

As well as being fun, a date where your aim is to sample the best your city has to offer doesn't allow for many awkward silent moments. Finished your course? You're off to your next destination! Best yet, you can tailor this date to suit your budget. When you find a restaurant you and your date like, suggest that the two of you return for a full meal. And—voilà!—you're all set for a follow-up date.

Choose restaurants near one another, especially if you intend to walk or take public transportation.

After each stop, pull out a notebook and rate each restaurant according to atmosphere, service, and fare.

Big Spender Version

Here's your chance to wine and dine your sweetheart. Pull out all the stops and visit the most talked-about restaurants in your city. Add wine tasting to your progressive dinner for added flare.

SharpNote

This date may have too many stops for a first date, where sometimes getting through one course can be hard enough. Save this one for the third or fourth outing.

Required Gear

A big appetite.

The Radio DJ Date

The Date

Grace a local radio station with a guest appearance.

Why It's Great

Broadcasting your opinions and expertise is fun, simply because you know others are listening. Listening to your date on the radio can reveal information you didn't know about her and may lead to other "off the record" conversations.

College radio stations provide the best shot at being a guest. Most shows offer music, but some also feature news and public-affairs programming. Try pitching the radio DJ about broadcasting your how-to advice for last-minute final exam cramming or your insight as to which classes best prepare students for the working world. A sure radio winner is to take callers with dating questions—while you're on a date of your own.

Another way to hit the airwaves is by contacting a low-power radio station. These stations have a short broadcast range but can be even more creative with their programming choices.

Big Spender Version

Many large radio stations sell blocks of airtime in the late-night and early-morning hours. Many companies buy these blocks for infomercials. Why not purchase airtime for your own radio show? Contact the sales department of your local talk or music station and inquire about buying a block of time. Consult with your date about the "format" of your show and get on the air!

SharpNote

The Big Spender Version is not advised for first dates.

Required Gear

No gear required; this date is all about winging it!

Chapter Three

Great Dates Daytime

The Good Thing Date

The Date

An afternoon (or evening) of arts and crafts, with brown-bag picnic or takeout thrown in.

Why It's Great

Most people enjoy spending an afternoon working on a craft project. It's relaxing, fun, conducive to easy conversation, and smacks of the kind of cool stuff we all used to love doing as kids. Since busy lives prevent most women from indulging in these projects, a date devoted to crafts may seem downright *decadent*. Best yet, you can have this date almost anywhere and at any time of year: at your house, at her house, at a park table on a nice day, or in the common area of your dormitory.

You can choose the project yourself from a magazine like *Martha Stewart Living* or *Real Simple* and have all of the supplies ready when you pick up your date. Alternatively, consider letting her choose the project and heading over to the art store together.

Big Spender Version

Want to make yourself irreplaceable? Soar beyond basic craft territory and straight into the "honey-do" promised land. Plan a date to fix, hang, update, replace, or remodel some or all of the things that have been bugging your woman around her place. Make a list in advance. Plan to buy all the materials—screws, nails, hangers, 3-in-1 oil, duct tape—you know the drill. Oh yeah, and don't forget the drill, tape measure, level, and other assorted handyman tools. When you factor in either the cost of a professional handyman or your hourly rate, you will have a Big Spender date in no time.

SharpNote

Gauge your companion before choosing this date.

Required Gear

A magazine or craft idea book and the supplies required for your chosen activity. Don't forget to tell your date to wear comfortable clothing.

The Sensitive Guy Date

The Date

Offer to take out your woman and her favorite little person for a day at the park, carnival, or other child-friendly venue. Include lunch at a hot-dog stand or other easy snack spot.

Why It's Great

This great date is a good way to ingratiate yourself with a woman who just can't get enough of that certain little someone. High points of this great date include built-in entertainment and conversation courtesy of the kid, and built-in goodwill at having suggested the date in the first place (that's right, you're a "giver"). Even better, you can plan this date so that it costs as little (day at the park) or as much (amusement park) as you can afford. And while you'll have to fork out cash to feed three mouths rather than two, remember that kids are *designed* to eat on the cheap: In other words, three at the park can eat more cheaply than two at Chez Big Bucks.

Big Spender Version

First, upgrade the grub. Suggest fried chicken or pizza over the standard hot dog. Then think collectibles: commemorative photos, charcoal portraits, her and her kid's name in hieroglyphics, personalized hats, sweatshirts, mugs—things to remind her of this magical day. And if that's not enough, think about upgrading to a season pass so you and your group can return.

SharpNote

Get mom's permission before suggesting an activity to her child.

Required Gear

Comfortable clothing and whatever the child may require.

The Flea Market Date

The Date

A day of browsing through flea-market finds and someone else's castaways, combined with lunch or snacks and an early dinner.

Why It's Great

For starters, it's a unique date. Chances are the last guy who took her out didn't think of this. Second, hunting for stuff at a flea market or antique shop has all the earmarks of adventure. You never know what you might find or what will stimulate interesting conversation. One or both of you is likely to recognize an item from childhood, leading to a good story and more of an opportunity to get to know each other and establish a connection. Finally, a flea-market date is about that whole "nesting" thing (lining your nest with stuff required to make a "home"), which is bound to make you appear attractively stable to most women. Be generous with the hot pretzels and lemonade or coffee—browsing is hard work! Don't resist the urge (and opportunity) to score points by buying her a small knickknack when she's not looking—a nice memento of your great date. Throw in lunch or dinner, and you've got a winner.

Big Spender Version

Think bigger than knickknacks and go for something she drooled over. A table or unique chair. A mirror or picture frame. Something *made* for her and her home. Alternatively, consider picking up something that needs your serious T.L.C. to bring it back to life. Buy it for her with the promise that you will refinish, restore, or otherwise revamp it to be a personal, one-of-a-kind memory of a most unique date.

SharpNote

To find a flea market in your area, check your local newspaper's classified section. Alternatively, ask local merchants for an area with lots of small antique stores—they usually settle in patches. Many cities also have "antique malls," warehouses that rent retail space to collectibles vendors. Look for antique dealers in your local newspapers.

Required Gear

Don't forget good walking shoes, cash (many vendors don't take plastic), and sunglasses, hats, or jackets, depending on the season.

The Go-karting! Date

The Date

A day (or evening) spent at a go-kart park, complete with hot dogs, sodas, and compliments on her racing skills.

Why It's Great

Some kids have all the luck. You remember the ones who always seemed to have their dads around to take them on camping trips, to amusement parks, and to the ball game? Yeah, ours wasn't around either—but you can make up for all that now! Go-karting is one of those activities that you probably always wanted to do as a kid, but never got to (or never got enough of). Believe it or not, most women long for those days when "girls'" activities weren't so different from what the boys did. Plus, any activity that allows adults to act like children is guaranteed to deliver a good time. This date is also a natural conversation starter.

Big Spender Version

Kick go-karting up a notch by renting an exotic car or motorcycle for the day. Then let your hair down and tool around, perfecting the windblown look. Oh yeah, and don't forget to let her drive—at least a little bit.

SharpNote

Don't let that competitive edge get the better of you. This is a *date*, so be sure to compliment her driving and avoid gloating about acing out her lap times. The cost of this activity is higher than a stroll through the park, but you make up the difference by being generous with the snack food.

Find a local go-kart park in the Yellow Pages or go online. Many are located on the outskirts of town, allowing for a nice drive and some time to talk.

Required Gear

Remember comfortable clothing and shoes and plenty of quarters for the arcade games.

The Brunch and a Walk Date

The Date

A great midmorning weekend meal and a walk through a park, commercial area, or residential neighborhood.

Why It's Great

Most guys overlook this winner, but it's simple and it *reeks* of romance. Why? There's something decadent about eating a lazy Saturday or Sunday brunch. It's a "special occasion" when you can enjoy food slowly—while the sun is still out—without having to rush back to a dimly lit workspace. Be choosy about your restaurant. Pick a place with a great view of water, mountains, or passersby. Set the tone by ordering something you would have only on a leisurely weekend. Chances are she'll follow your lead.

Top off a good meal with a romantic walk around an attractive residential area, a not-too-bustling commercial area, or a park, and you've got all the makings for relaxed conversation and romance. It's simple, but it works.

Big Spender Version

Check out resort areas near your town. Many hotels and bed-and-breakfast establishments have lavish weekend buffets. Then, pump the date up even more by calling ahead and ordering her favorite flowers delivered to the ideal table.

SharpNote

A great first date. Also perfect for a last-minute date with that great woman you just met the night before, or when one or both of you are unavailable during the evenings.

Required Gear

Comfortable clothing and a good pair of shoes.

The Pampering Date

The Date

A day at a spa, with massages or other spa treatments for both of you, followed by lunch.

Why It's Great

Women dig spas. Period. Why, you ask? Because it doesn't suck to have someone pampering you for several hours—it just doesn't. This spa date may not be the cheapest date on our list, but it doesn't have to be the most expensive. Spa treatment prices range by facility, so look around for a service provider that matches your budget. Often "day spas" and even some "destination spas" (where you stay the night) that are located farther away from town have better prices than the ones paying high urban rents. If you choose to book a spa that's an hour or two out of town, you'll have the added benefit of a nice car ride, a longer date, and the feeling that you've "gotten away."

Start by booking massages. Many facilities offer tandem massages, where you and your date enjoy massages in the same room, side by side. If your budget allows, schedule a facial or a manicure/pedicure treatment for her, as well. Looking for something different? Try a salt rub—a vigorous massage using coarse grains of salt to remove dead skin cells.

Follow up your day at the spa's restaurant or another place serving relatively light fare.

Big Spender Version

The saying goes something like this: *If you give a man a fish, he eats for a day. Teach him to fish, and you'll feed a whole village.* I know, we're talking about massages here, not fish. But hang in and you'll see where this is going. If you want to put your money where it will garner the biggest payoff, think about hiring a massage therapist who gives lessons. She (or he) can teach you how to massage your date and then teach your date how to massage you in return. Learn a few key techniques and you'll never have to fish for a compliment again.

SharpNote

While no woman will say no to a spa first date, don't do it. Spa time is personal, intimate, and can be pricey—not the ideal icebreaker.

Choose your spa and make appointments in advance—*well* in advance for more popular spas on busy weekends. Plan to show up at least half an hour early in order to enjoy the cool locker rooms and decadent terrycloth robes.

Required Gear

You won't need anything for your time at the spa, as robes and slip-on shoes are generally provided. However, since this is a date, consider bringing along your toiletry kit for post-massage grooming (massages tend to mess up your hair). Suggest that your date do the same.

The Hands-on Date

The Date

Spend the day on a hands-on project. Add lunch or an early dinner.

Why It's Great

Yeah, we thought the "hands-on" part of the date title would get your attention—now get your mind out of the gutter, big guy. As with the Good Thing Date (page 82), you'll find that spending time working on something together is entertaining and different, and provides plenty of opportunity for easy conversation. In recent years, ceramic painting has made a big splash, with tons of storefronts making it easy for you and your date to pick, paint, and fire your own ceramic objects. Forget that—it's been done. Instead, pick another hands-on activity—painting, drawing, actual clay molding (or "throwing"), even winemaking from an at-home kit—that allows the two of you to spend some time up close and personal.

Big Spender Version

Find an artist you both like and hire him or her to school you in his style of work. You buy the start-up medium—paint, clay, papier-mâché, canvas, or whatever. Let her pick the artist and the location for the lessons.

SharpNote

A great first date, or a date for the guy who's been getting some pressure for a romantic date from his longtime woman.

Required Gear

Gear is largely dependent on the project you choose. Check out community centers and other places that provide instruction in art and hands-on projects. If you choose to use these facilities, most of the materials will be provided. Alternatively, check out hobby shops, children's shops, or "discovery shops," where beermaking, winemaking, and other unusual home-project kits are sold. Work clothes are advised.

The Factory Tour Date

The Date

Tour a regional beer, bread, candy, or fudge factory, with plenty of free samples along the way, followed by some real food, as needed.

Why It's Great

Talk about taking the pressure off of you! This date provides plenty of entertaining distraction *and* opportunity for conversation. It's a great way to learn about something new, including your date's likes and dislikes. Nothing to say? Comment on what you're looking at, tasting, or hearing.

The key is to choose the right tour. Remember, you are courting *her*, so pick a venue that interests her. If she's not a beer drinker, forget the brewsky tour. On the other hand, if she has a favorite regional candy brand, loves the smell of fresh bread (and is not a no-carb dieter), or loves a certain brand of soda made locally, she'll appreciate a date designed around her personal passion. Of course, factory tours are not limited to the production of food. Old-style papermaking facilities or furniture makers may sound kind of dull to you but would appeal to a traditionalist. For a woman who can't live without her BlackBerry, an electronics producer might be the thrill of a lifetime. Figure out her passion and plan a day around learning about what interests her.

If you choose a food-oriented tour, plan to eat at the tail end of the date. Touring a fudge factory on a full stomach is a bad idea. Additionally, a post-tour lunch has the added benefit of guaranteeing that you'll have something to talk about.

Big Spender Version

Often the factory your date chooses to tour features a type of product that's near and dear to her heart. After touring the facility, why not continue the fun of this date by bringing some of the company back home with you? Sure, most Big Spenders won't be able to buy the whole factory, but almost anyone can purchase shares in a publicly traded company. Pick up a few shares prior to your outing and present your date with the stock certificates—and a copy of the *Wall Street Journal*—while dining at a business-district eatery following your tour.

SharpNote

Most factories offer tours during the week. Weekend tours are often available for those who phone ahead. Call around to see what's available in your area. Ideally, try to find a tour that's more than an hour long. You want to see the good stuff.

Required Gear

Comfortable shoes are a good idea. Call ahead to determine if warm clothing is required, as most production facilities are temperature controlled.

The Casual Pool Date

The Date

Spend an afternoon (or evening) shooting pool.

Why It's Great

For a very casual get-to-know-you afternoon date, the pool hall is gold. Pool gives you the opportunity to show off your skills (or lack thereof), compliment her strategy, and enjoy easy conversation. It seems that *no one* holds back any secrets in these places.

Consider checking out the pool hall before you suggest this date. Make sure it's a classy place, not a dingy dive that'll reflect poorly on you. Buy her a drink, and after you've finished your game, offer to take her for coffee or a snack. Show her a great time here, and she'll look forward to having you ask her out on a "big" date.

Big Spender Version

Take your pool date from casual to serious. Begin by purchasing pool cues for you and your woman. Then look into joining a pool league through the American Poolplayers Association (APA). Visit www.poolplayers.com on the Internet and get more information on weekly pool leagues in your area. Finally, throw in a subscription to *Pool & Billiard* magazine (www.poolmag.com) for a date that keeps on giving.

SharpNote

Great for a first date, a last-minute date, or an afternoon out with a longtime companion.

Required Gear

Unless you own your own cue stick, no special gear is required.

The Hunting and Gathering Date

The Date

Spend a morning or afternoon hunting for stuff—shells, rocks, or flowers. Add a picnic lunch, weather permitting, or a casual meal at a nearby lunch spot.

Why It's Great

Most humans enjoy collecting. This date incorporates the fun of finding something cool with two important great date elements: a subtle sense of date "adventure" and easy, obvious topics of conversation. Plus, when planned right, a hunting-and-gathering date reeks of romance—at a nice price.

Figure out what your date would enjoy and what your surroundings offer. Shell collecting doesn't necessarily require a beach. Many inland areas (and we mean way, *way* inland) are rich with fossilized shells and evidence of past sea life. Quite cool, actually.

Depending on how into it your date gets, you can pair this excursion with a plan for a follow-up date to use your natural finds in a joint craft project (see the Good Thing Date, page 82). This is an easy way to turn one great date into a second.

Big Spender Version

There's hunting and gathering in nature, and then there's the hunting and gathering that urban folk do . . . shopping! Sadly, many of us happily buy for others and scrimp when it comes to ourselves. Has your long-term honey held off on buying something that she requires? Insist on taking her out to collect the thing she's sure she *can* live without. Whether it's a pair of shoes, a new CD, or a new printer, make a special day of it. Insist that today is your day to pamper *her*. Follow up with a romantic meal and conversation, so you can "gather" new information about the woman you love.

SharpNote

Only the modest version of this date is appropriate for first outings.

Required Gear

Comfortable walking shoes are always a good bet. Depending on the season, jackets or sun hats may also be in order. Don't forget to bring along a couple of beach pails or daypacks for holding and hiking out your finds. Consider throwing in a reference book on the rocks, shells, or flowers you'll be collecting; finding out more about the stuff you've found makes for great conversation. Finally, pack a picnic lunch, complete with picnic blanket and drinks—a nice romance topper.

The Test Drive Date

The Date

Spend an afternoon picking out and test driving her choice of dream cars. Precede with lunch or follow with an early dinner.

Why It's Great

Duh. Everyone has a dream car, and most of us never get anywhere near the wheel. Why not spend the afternoon checking out and getting into the set of wheels of her dreams? Lots to talk about and even more to keep her interest level up. A great opportunity to get to know your date and to compliment her taste and her driving—a winner.

The key to making this date work is focusing on the kinds of cars *she* likes; in other words, this one isn't about you. Pick up a few brochures prior to the date. Over lunch or on the way over, ask her about her dream car and ask her if she'd like to drive one. Show her the brochures and choose a few other models to round out the day. In most cities and rural areas, automobile dealerships are located on the same street or within the same "auto mall," making it easy to do the rounds. Assuming you're not thinking Ferrari or Maserati, most salespeople will be happy to let your date get behind the wheel.

Start with lunch, a great time to peruse the brochures and determine your first pit stop, or follow with dinner.

Big Spender Version

While a test drive can be fun, if you really want to wring out a car, look into renting her dream car for the day. Then pick a restaurant two hours away. Don't forget to bring along the tunes and a road map (seriously). And be sure to let her drive at least one way.

SharpNote

Great for first dates.

Required Gear

Car brochures, if you have time to pick them up; these will help get her over her initial hesitation. Aside from that, all you need is the confident look of a potential buyer....

The "I Will Plant You a Garden" Date

The Date

Spend the afternoon showing off (or faking) your green thumb as you plan and plant a city garden for your date's apartment. Add lunch from a nearby takeout spot.

Why It's Great

Women love handy guys. There's just something about a guy who can get stuff done that translates into "keeper" in her mind. Why not incorporate some of this magic into your next afternoon out? Planning and planting a "city garden" for her apartment is conducive to easy conversation and provides built-in entertainment—it's also a relaxing way to get to know your date.

Know nothing about plants? No problem. Pick up a home gardening book and check out the basics. When you pick up your date, let her know what you have in mind and head over to the nursery.

If you don't have time to read up, the folks at the nursery can help you with whatever you don't know about plants. Be sure to iet them know whether you're planting an indoor or outdoor garden and how much sun the area gets. Get a few attractive pots or planter boxes and some soil and get back to her place. Spread out newspapers or work outside to avoid a big cleanup. Order lunch from a local delivery joint and sit back and enjoy her new garden. She'll love it.

Big Spender Version

With a little homework you can ramp this date up while making it look easy. Go beyond a mere garden and consider a total "outdoor space makeover." Add a garden bench and picket fence to a swath of wildflowers, and you have a

Victorian garden. A minimalist birdbath, some smooth stones, and sleek greenery reflects a Zen aesthetic. Inquire as to her taste in garden design and go all the way with it.

SharpNote

This date is on the generous side, and therefore is not recommended for a first-time outing.

Required Gear

You can pick up the plants, containers, and potting soil at the nursery you visit. Because purchasing the materials is part of the date *you* planned, we suggest you spring for the stuff. After all, you would have paid for the movie or other activity, right? Plus, it's a little awkward to say, "Hey, I've got this great idea, now cough up some money for it." You get the picture.

The Great Trade Show Date

The Date

Spend a day at a trade show checking out stuff she likes—a lot of it. Include lunch, an early dinner, or both.

Why It's Great

Most of us have hobbies. When you plan a date around *her* pet interest and an insider's view of the industry behind it, you've got another winner. Does your date like stamps, books, gadgets, collectible miniatures, or dogs? There's likely to be a trade show in town that caters to one of these. Aren't you sweet to focus on her hobby? Yes you are. *Next time we'll have to go to a show that* you *like.* Uh, yes we will.

Just think of it: she'll be so engrossed in all that trade show stuff that no matter *what* you say, you're bound to seem interesting and charming. Throw in plenty of event snacks—hot pretzels, sodas, hot dogs—and you'll be "generous" too.

Big Spender Version

Most trade shows have speaker conferences that require an additional entrance fee. Since you and your date are already getting your feet wet on the topic, consider total immersion and spring for the private, extra, or specific speaker functions. Come prepared with notepads, pens, or a mini tape recorder, if allowed.

SharpNote

This date works best for third dates and beyond, since all the activity makes conversation and connection a bit more difficult.

To find a trade show in your region, check the local papers or go online. The entrance fee may be a bit pricey, but realize that this gets you an entire *day* of entertainment. If you're still hungry after all those trade-show snacks, add a light dinner.

Required Gear

Walking shoes, definitely. Those long trade-show aisles will wear your loafers into the ground; same for her. You're likely to get a freebie bag when you walk in, but in case you don't, bring along a daypack for collecting pamphlets and samples. For extra points, offer to carry hers.

The Charitable Guy Date

The Date

Spend the day volunteering your time with a charity of your or her choosing. Throw in lunch or an early dinner.

Why It's Great

Women dig it when you're philanthropic. If you want to earn "nice guy" points, this is the way to go. But on a date? Sure, why not?

Most charitable events require you to work in groups, allowing you and your date to work side by side, wrapping gifts for children, decorating and setting up a charity event, or working the phone lines at your local public radio station's funding drive. You'll get great conversation and an opportunity to show what a swell guy you are—all for *free*.

At the end of a shift, many organizations provide food for their volunteers. This is where your moochery should end, big guy. Thank everyone, grab your date, and take her out for a meal alone.

Big Spender Version

They say charity begins at home. The Big Spender version of this date allows you to do the most good. Step up and volunteer your home for use as a fund-raising venue. In most instances the charity will take care of all the details. It's win-win. You become a major benefactor—with your date on your arm—and your charity of choice gets a much-needed financial boost.

SharpNote

You can find a worthwhile cause by searching the classifieds, listening to the radio, or inquiring at a local church, synagogue, mosque, or community center. Avoid events that are too heart-wrenching; remember, this *is* a date.

Required Gear

Consult with the organizer of the event you choose.

The Flower Market Date

The Date

Take a tour of your local wholesale flower market, followed by a late breakfast or lunch.

Why It's Great

Most women love getting flowers. Unfortunately, a lot of florists charge an arm and a leg to pick, arrange, and wrap your choice of stems. Why not go to the source? Most towns have a wholesale flower market where flower suppliers showcase and sell a wide assortment of flowers to the trade. After a certain hour, these markets generally open to the public.

The key to this date is timing; the early bird catches the worm. Most flower markets open at 6 a.m. and open to the public after 8 a.m. Plan to pick up your date—coffee in hand—at around that time and head down to the market. You'll wander through stalls, checking out a wide assortment of flowers sold in bunches.

Treat your date to a few bunches of her favorite types—remember, the prices are *wholesale*. If you've ever considered filling up a woman's apartment with countless bunches of flowers, this is your chance to do it on the cheap.

Stash the flowers in your car and take in a late breakfast or early lunch. Then head back to her place and help her arrange the haul. Insist she keep the majority, if not all.

Big Spender Version

Sadly, the beauty of cut flowers is fleeting. Looking for something that will last? There *is* a way to use flowers to communicate your longer-term intentions. While on your date at the flower market, ask her to pick out the flowering plants that catch her eye. Ideally, look for varieties that are large and flowering at the moment. The more fragrant, the better. After your date, set aside time to plant or arrange for the planting of these beauties in a place where she can't miss them. If your date doesn't have a yard, patio, or balcony, look around her neighborhood for a spot she passes daily. Most schools and churches will gladly accept a donation of flowering plants. Condition your donation on a planting location where your date will see your thoughtfulness on her daily commute.

SharpNote

Ask around about the wholesale flower district in your town. If you live in a more remote location, flowers are often delivered and sold from trucks arriving from bigger cities nearby.

Required Gear

Bring a couple of canvas bags to the market for easy transport of the flowers you buy—these will save you trips back to the car. Florists head out to market with water-filled buckets in their cars in order to keep the flowers fresh en route. You can do the same by bringing along a couple of buckets and bottles of water, then wedge the water-filled buckets and flowers between your front and back seats for the ride home. Consider bringing along a few garbage bag liners and a couple of rags—just in case.

The Date on Wheels

The Date

Spend a day or afternoon biking, in-line skating, or roller-skating in the park or on a boardwalk.

Why It's Great

As with the Fair Date (page 34), this date sounds totally cheesy until you try it. There's something about being out on a nice day that makes any date work. You always end up asking yourself "Why don't I do this *every* weekend?" When executed properly, you can bet your date will be asking herself the same question about *you*.

Start by picking a nice location for the day's events. On weekends with good weather, parks and other public areas often host art fairs or other events; check your local paper to ensure that an event won't get in the way of your plans (wheels and breakable objects don't mix well).

However, if neither of you have mastered roller-skating or blading, consider biking instead. It's one thing for you to be helping her along, but it's quite another for your poor skating to be holding her back or—worse—requiring her to take you to the emergency room.

Plan to hit a lunch spot about halfway through your route.

Big Spender Version

Want to roll with a little more dough? Park your car at one end of the beach, boardwalk, or park and do your rolling thing one way, secure in the knowledge that you have a cab or—even better—a limo on its way to pick you up at the end of your roll.

If it's a limo, definitely ride to lunch or dinner, or enjoy an air-conditioned cruise through town, complete with nibbles and drinks for the trip.

SharpNote

Beaches and other shorelines generally have stands with rental bikes; bike shops also offer rentals. Roller- and in-line skates may be rented by the hour at many parks and shops. Look into rental options prior to your date.

Required Gear

Good shoes are a must, but cycling shoes aren't. Comfortable clothing, a windproof jacket, sunglasses, sunscreen, and helmets are also recommended. Make sure to bring along a couple bottles of water or prepare to stop for refreshments—your treat.

The Sandcastle Date

The Date

Spend an afternoon building the home of your dreams—out of sand, of course.

Why It's Great

Again, anything you do to bring out the kid in her will generally be well received. Taking the time to build something together will give you plenty to talk and joke about—and the price is right.

Best yet, building a sandcastle doesn't require a sandy beach. If you live inland, consider scoping out a sandbox at a local park. There's no need to kick out the playing kids; just dive in and slowly take over the joint.

Follow up your engineering feat with a picnic lunch, complete with blanket. A walk after lunch is always nice.

Big Spender Version

On a date this simple, ramping up to Big Spender is not easy, but it can be done. Contact a local sculptor or art student from the art department of the college in your town. Arrange for him or her to design and help you and your date execute the *ultimate* sandcastle! For even more effect, call an upscale caterer or event planner and arrange for a complete, catered fantasy meal on the beach. This can (and should) include not only exquisite food, but a canopy, real table and chairs, china, silver, crystal, and champagne. This Big Spender version is too intimidating for a first date, but may be an ideal "getaway" when the air between you and your companion has begun to crackle with electricity.

SharpNote

Only the modest version of this date is appropriate for a first date.

Required Gear

You'll be erecting the world's greatest sandcastle, so bring all that you need—think sand tools and stuff from around the house for fine detail work. Don't forget a sand pail or bucket (include bottled water if you're headed to a park). Tell your date to wear comfortable clothes. Don't forget that the knees of blue jeans tend to fade after you grind them into wet sand for a few hours.

Consider packing a digital or Polaroid camera for recording your handiwork. Photos make for a great keepsake.

The Fisherman's Date

The Date

Spend the day (or evening) fishing for your lunch or dinner.

Why It's Great

Sure fish reek, but they taste pretty good. For guys who enjoy casting a lure with their buddies, why not do the same with a date? A day of fishing gives you something to do, something to talk about, and a nice follow-up activity: eating.

Choose a local lake or pier known for good fishing. Crank up the tunes and offer your date her choice of refreshments as you await (and hopefully catch) your dinner. Once you reel 'em in, head over to a local fish house and ask the chef to prepare the fish as you request. Add a few side dishes and drinks, and you'll have a meal to remember.

No luck fishing? Hit a local market, pick up some fresh fish, discard the market wrapping, and head over to the restaurant, anyway. Silly, sure, but you'll get a laugh out of your date and a few points for trying. Make it your "little secret."

Big Spender Version

Bring 'em home alive...the fish, that is. Consider doing your "fishing" at a local exotic fish and aquarium store. Depending on her interest, invite your date to choose the aquarium setup, including pump, gravel, castle, and exotic fish. *Really* Big Spenders will make it a saltwater tank. Is she worried about the upkeep? Spring for the cost of monthly tank maintenance visits until she feels comfortable caring for the tank herself.

SharpNote

No idea where to take your catch? Many piers and waterfront areas are close to seafood restaurants that are willing to prepare your local catch. Most chefs enjoy the challenge and will be happy to oblige, especially if you call to arrange the meal ahead of the date.

Don't spring this outing on a woman who might find fishing or aquariums cruel.

Required Gear

Comfortable clothes, fishing gear, and bait. Two small coolers: one for drinks and a second one for your catch. Also consider a small portable radio and sun hats and sunglasses as needed.

Some piers and lakes have stands that rent fishing equipment. Call ahead.

The Beach Blanket BBQ Date

The Date

Plan a beach barbecue—whether or not you intend to hit the water.

Why It's Great

Time together on a beach spells r-o-m-a-n-c-e. If you're gonna go out to lunch, anyway, why not combine it with a little beach-romance time?

Stake out the seaside or lakefront beach you'd like to visit. Check to see if fires are permitted.

For your meal, get the good, fancy stuff that goes beyond burgers and dogs. Try fresh fish wrapped in foil with a few lemon slices and olive oil thrown in. It's not a big deal if you have the fish market clean the fillet for you. Throw in the lemons and oil and wrap tightly. Done. Cut up some veggies (long, thick, flat pieces that cook easily but won't fall through the grill); add olive oil, salt, and pepper, and throw it all in a Ziploc bag. Also bring wine and dessert.

When you're ready to grill, toss the foil-wrapped fish on the fire and arrange the vegetables on the grill. The fish will take about 15–20 minutes—and the veggies about half that time. Watch both to avoid burning. Then sit back and enjoy your meal and the company of your date.

Big Spender Version

Go gourmet. Check out the meat section of a high-end grocery store or butcher shop. Ask for assistance in choosing and preparing exotic meat. You and your date can learn how to cook fire-roasted pheasant with mango-papaya salsa or throw on some ostrich burgers. Your butcher will guide you through the most rare and exotic stock, in addition to giving you explicit instructions on how to barbecue your meat in style.

SharpNote

Weather permitting, this date also works well at dinnertime. Call ahead to ensure that limited beach hours won't get you kicked out before the fun begins and that fires are permitted after sundown.

Required Gear

Tell your date to wear warm clothing or a swimsuit (depending on the weather and time of day). Pack two blankets (one for covering up when cold), a couple of pillows for leaning back on, and some drinking water. Add candles (and something to protect them from the wind, like a hurricane glass), plates, cups, and silverware—the real stuff looks much better. Bring a portable radio for some tunes.

If your beach doesn't have grilling facilities, pick up a small portable grill at any major drugstore chain or hardware store. Don't forget charcoal (get the mesquite kind for a nice smell), lighter fluid, and matches.

The Where the #%$@ Are We? Date

The Date

Plan a day that takes you and your date to a new part of town. Include a meal, preferably one representative of that locale.

Why It's Great

Adventure is an important element of any great date. Show her a fun—and different—time, and you'll score points. Does this "adventure" require a trip abroad? No way. Why not check out a not-often-explored part of your own town? Chances are, there are parts of the city where you live that neither of you have ever seen. Plan a day or evening of exploration. Take out the map and locate interesting historic venues, shopping districts and, of course, unknown eateries. Use a good local restaurant guide (such as the Zagat Survey) to pick an eatery and work from there.

A variation on this is the "Point at the Map" Date. Pick up a local map and have your date point to any area where she's never been. With your trusty restaurant guide in hand (and perhaps a local tourist guidebook), pick an eatery from which to begin your adventure, then use the guidebook to find sites or shops in that area.

Big Spender Version

Rather than simply visiting an unknown place for the day, pick up a local inn guide along with your map. Meet with your date the night before your planned adventure, ask her to pick a point on the map, and then book an evening's stay at a romantic inn for the following night.

SharpNote

The modest version of this great date requires almost no preplanning, since it's all done with your date! The Big Spender version requires an evening of phone calls. The overnight version of this date may not be appropriate for first and early dates.

Required Gear

A restaurant guide is a must. A tourist guidebook for your town is also a good idea. You'll be surprised by what you didn't know. Good walking shoes are advised, as are jackets in cooler weather.

The Walk in the Woods Date

The Date

This daytime date includes some exercise and a great picnic.

Why It's Great

Most of us forget how good we feel after spending the day outside—it's relaxing *and* memorable. Why not make it a date? Consider planning a day of hiking or vigorous walking. Many towns and regions have hiking parks or trails accessible to day hikers. Ask around or pick up a regional hiking guidebook to find a trailhead near you. You'll have plenty to talk about while you walk behind her and admire the great, uh, *view*.

Pack a picnic lunch and stow it in a backpack. Finger foods work best and provide for easy cleanup and pack-out. She'll love it, and you'll look like a guy who understands how to create great romance in the great outdoors.

Big Spender Version

Nearly all rustic areas offer trails, springs, waterfalls, and other picturesque features. And then there are the *secret* attractions known only to locals. Consider treating your date to a day of discovery. Contact a local business near the trailhead where you intend to walk or hike, ask for the names of local outdoor tour guides, and arrange to meet one—picnic in hand—for a very special tour of the area. Commemorate the date by making a donation to an eco-group in your date's name.

SharpNote

Because walking in the woods often brings you to remote locations, this date may make women who don't know you very well uncomfortable and may not be suitable for first dates.

Required Gear

Suitable shoes and clothes are a must. Hats, sunscreen, and bug repellent are also a great idea, as are warmer layers in the cooler months. Don't forget your backpack with lunch and cool drinks. Water works better than sugary beverages.

The History in the Making Date

The Date

Plan a day trip around a historical reenactment and local grub.

Why It's Great

Got a history buff on your hands? Make her hobby work for you. Consider planning a date around one of the many historical reenactments put on by history buffs just like your date. She'll dig getting up close and personal with subject matter she enjoys, and you'll get points for having suggested it. Add a local lunch, and you're guaranteed to get glowing reviews.

Big Spender Version

Dates like this always generate a lot of conversation—which is good—but the conversation inevitably leads to questions about who, when, where, and why. Big Spenders may wish to visit their local bookstore for a DVD on the historical event (perfect for a predate research night in) or a cassette or CD set for the ride over to the reenactment. The History Channel and PBS have produced many fine series on historical events, many released in boxed sets—a great souvenir for your date.

SharpNote

Know nothing about the event that you'll be attending? We suggest a brief online search to fill you in on crucial facts and provide a few points of trivia to serve as conversation starters.

How do you learn about historical reenactments in your area? Again, online searches are your best bet. Alternatively, call up or pay an online visit to your regional tourist board.

Required Gear

Call ahead to inquire about gear needed for local weather and terrain. Don't forget your camera.

The Bull's-eye Date

The Date

Spend an afternoon learning or—better yet—*teaching* your date a few of the finer points of archery. Finish off with lunch or dinner.

Why It's Great

Any guy who has ever had the opportunity to teach his date anything as cozy as archery can tell you the benefits of this date. Just imagine: You, getting up close behind your student as you impart important information about stance and aim; her, appreciative of your patience and strong physique. Starting to get it? A great way to get to know each other while you interest her in your interest.

Even if she has no desire to proceed with archery, this will be an entertaining and memorable date. Add lunch, an early dinner, or—even better—a picnic in the same spot where you put down your bow and arrow or at a local park. Archery ranges are generally run by the park service.

Big Spender Version

Hit the bull's-eye every time by hiring a pro to give you and your date the inside edge on this sport. Check at a local park or recreation area or even a local college for someone who wouldn't mind picking up a few bucks to show you the finer points.

SharpNote

A great first date for those who like to spend time outdoors, but aren't super athletic. After all, archery is a lot like bowling—a sport that requires skill, but not much physical endurance!

Required Gear

Archery equipment. Many archery ranges and archery-related stores allow you to rent gear.

The Dr. Science Date

The Date

Spend an afternoon at a local science museum. Add lunch or an early dinner.

Why It's Great

The cool thing about a science museum is that you get to play with stuff—lots of stuff. Talk about an interactive date! You'll have plenty to do and even more to talk about. Plus, you'll get points for taking her on a date that's part cultural, part educational, and *entirely* different.

Don't forget to visit the gift shop before you leave. Consider getting your date a small memento of your afternoon—the sillier the better. Then head over to a late lunch or early dinner place that's not too far from the museum; all that fun is likely to make a girl hungry.

Big Spender Version

A great date is all about chemistry. Ready to be your own mad scientist? Many high-end department stores feature fragrance counters lined with scores of essential oils that allow you to mix your own unique scent combinations for perfume or cologne. Spend an afternoon at one of these counters, alternating between sniffing fragrance notes and coffee beans (to refresh your sense of smell between scents) and treat your honey to a gift as unique as your time together. Among the woodsy, citrus, and spicy scents, you're bound to find something she'll love. Alternatively, visit your local bookstore for a title on scents and essential-oil combinations, follow that with a trip to a botanical or craft store for exotic oils and fragrance extracts, and do the mixing on your own....

SharpNote

The science museum is a great first-date idea.

Call ahead to ensure that the museum is open on the day you plan to visit. As museums are generally located in areas of the city most of us don't visit regularly, find and reserve a place for lunch or dinner prior to picking up your date.

Required Gear

Comfortable shoes are recommended.

The High Tea Date

The Date

Skip lunch and dinner and plan a "high tea."

Why It's Great

Women love this. There's just something about the English tradition of fueling up with caffeine, cakes, and tiny sandwiches that says, "I'm livin' the life" to most women. Bank on this by planning a high tea of your own. Visit a local tea shop or bakery for loose tea leaves (along with milk and sugar), a tea strainer, finger sandwiches, and small pastries. Arrange a tablecloth, cups, saucers, and plates of tea snacks and add a small vase of flowers. Put on light music. Think "movie magic." When your date arrives, escort her to her seat and serve the tea. Don't forget to ask, "One lump or two?"

After tea, invite her for a stroll. She'll love it.

Big Spender Version

Most high-end hotels and the occasional bakery or café serve a high tea on the weekends, around 3 p.m. These events book early, so plan to make your reservation a couple of weeks in advance. If the hotel or café has a view, request a prime window seat when you call.

Be warned: This "light meal" includes more than just the beverage. Some teas consist of small but substantial sandwiches, a variety of desserts, *and* champagne, and can run you $25–$100 per person.

After tea, invite her for a stroll around the hotel grounds or around the neighborhood where the café is located.

SharpNote

Skip this one for the first date and save it for an afternoon when you really want to make good. Great for a date with a longtime companion.

Required Gear

High tea generally requires you to dress up a bit. Think business casual with a jacket.

The Farmers' Lunch Date

The Date

Spend a morning or afternoon shopping for fresh fruits, vegetables, meats, fish, and flowers at a local farmers' market, then head back home to prepare a great lunch or dinner.

Why It's Great

Anyone who's ever tasted food made from fresher-than-usual fruits and vegetables knows how much better it can be. And anyone who's ever had *really* great food on a date knows how much better date food can be. That's why this variation on the Home-cooked Meal Date (page 26) is so great. Start your day by picking up your date and heading over to a local farmers' market. Choose fresh stuff and inquire about what can be made from various items. Your date is sure to step in with suggestions. Don't forget the wine and flowers. Stop off at a grocery store for any additional dry goods you may need and head over to her place or yours. Prepare lunch or dinner as she watches in amazement or let her get in on the fun. Like the Home-cooked Meal Date, this great date is sure to please.

Big Spender Version

Ramp up the elegance of your meal with a recipe featuring pricey and difficult-to-find ingredients, like hundred-year-old eggs...shark's fin...truffles (the piggy kind)...and saffron. Go on the hunt to round them up. Your prize will be a unique and scrumptious meal back at your place.

SharpNote

Not ideal for the average first date, since many women may be uncomfortable "eating in" so early on.

Urban farmers' markets have become more popular in recent years. To find a farmers' market in your area, check your local paper or call a public radio station. Most markets open in the morning and close when vendors exhaust their inventory. Other markets open specifically for afternoon shopping.

Required Gear

Consider bringing along a couple of canvas bags to save trips back to the car. We suggest that you cover the cost of all the ingredients; after all, you would have picked up dinner, right?

The Historic Home Tour Date

The Date

Take a tour of beautiful historic homes to see how the other half lives...or to keep up with the Joneses....

Why It's Great

This date is not only easily accessible to most people, it also makes you look like you're cultured and know the town, even if you just looked up your activity in the phone book that day. Besides, it's a good idea to get to know your town's history and everything it has to offer, so you won't be a boring schmo. If there are simply no historic homes to tour in your town, there's doubtless something worth seeing within a half hour's drive. Look into it.

Big Spender Version

Sometimes historic homes or house museums offer extras to guests like carriage rides or exclusive reservation-only dinners, which are always quite romantic. The historic-home tour can also be easily paired with a nice dinner, or you can continue the cultural theme and check out a nearby museum.

SharpNote

Call the home ahead of time, as tours often start at specified hours, and it's always good to demonstrate that you did some planning. At some homes you might also need to make reservations. After your tour, check out the gift shop and drop a few bucks for a cheesy souvenir gift, along with a dollar or two in the donation box; historic homes are usually nonprofit, and your show of support will be appreciated.

Required Gear

One of the best things about this great date is that it doesn't require any additional gear.

The Dress Rehearsal Date

The Date

Ever wonder how theater companies get it all together for opening night? Treat your date to a sneak peak.

Why It's Great

This date is loads of fun. Get a glimpse of an upcoming play while it's *almost* ready for opening night, but technically still in rehearsal. Most theater companies have one or two rehearsal nights that are open to the public for a lesser charge, to give the actors and theater staff a chance to get accustomed to a small audience before the play actually premieres. This is your opportunity to enjoy all the bloopers and stage accidents that the regular audience won't see. Backdrop falls over? Wig comes off? Curtain accidentally closes in the middle of the scene? Perfect after-date chat fodder. You'll be talking about this one for a long time. And if everything goes smoothly, even better—you'll have gotten what everyone else is going to get, but for a smaller price tag.

Big Spender Version

Many theater companies are strapped for cash. Often a small donation can get you backstage with the cast. Call the company manager and arrange to bring your date into the action following the show!

SharpNote

This is a perfect date for students or those on a strict budget. Resist the temptation to pair this date with anything less theatrical, like a movie.

Required Gear

Bring a few bucks for the tickets, and that's it!

The Classic Car Date

The Date

Check out a classic car show.

Why It's Great

Ever checked out a classic car show? They're loads of fun, and most only charge entry fees to the people who bring their cars, not the people who come to view. These cars may be old, but they're far from junky; the care their owners lavish on them is amazing. You'll see cars from the 1940s classics to 1960s Mustangs to 1970s muscle cars and unique trucks. Even if your date is not an auto enthusiast, this outing will be fascinating.

Look for information on classic car shows online; they're a lot more common than you might think.

Big Spender Version

Live in a large city with a variety of restaurant choices? Pair this date with a trip to a 1950s-style diner, where you can enjoy hamburgers and milk shakes. Then go swing dancing. A hoot!

SharpNote

Classic-car owners take great pride in their refurbishing accomplishments and love it when you admire their "babies." Remember, look but don't touch, unless the owner says it's okay. A great first date.

Required Gear

Nothing but comfortable walking shoes are required, but consider doing some reading on cars of various eras prior to your date—that way you and your companion will be better able to appreciate what you see.

The Downward-facing Dog Date

The Date

Take your honey to a yoga class.

Why It's Great

Like golf, yoga is a great group activity that provides some insight into your companion's personality. Don't know what we mean? Just check out your date's and fellow yoga-goers' faces as they try to maneuver themselves into unusual poses, not to mention trying to balance themselves in the position, and it'll actually tell you a lot about how your date handles life's little frustrations and challenges. Does she take on the challenge with a smile or giggle? You've probably got a winner. On the other hand, if your date spends the class complaining or heaving heavy sighs, then you know you're with a *whiner*. Yoga is also tons of fun and great for your health. Have a light meal after your class.

Big Spender Version

For a splurge, treat your date to a massage after the workout, then go for smoothies and a scenic bike ride. Yoga also pairs wonderfully with a refreshing, light sushi dinner and sake. Or, if you'd like to stay with the whole yoga-Indian theme, go out for a curry or spicy vindaloo. Don't forget the breath mints if you'd like a good-night kiss!

SharpNote

If either you or your date has never done yoga before, make a point of choosing a beginners' class.

Required Gear

Loose-fitting workout clothes, yoga mats (often available at your yoga studio), a towel, and a change of clothes for lunch or dinner.

The Big Audition Date

The Date

Invite your date to join you for a local theater audition, for the ultimate make-a-fool-of-yourself-to-impress-your-date opportunity.

Why It's Great

Nearly everyone enjoys daydreams of being a star. This date idea allows you to give your date a chance to shine. Check out local theater listings to find small theater auditions in your area. Dare her to join you on an audition! Even if you and your date simply leave as acting legends in your own minds, she'll always remember this date for its hilarity. While this may not be a "romantic" activity, it's most definitely lighthearted and memorable.

Big Spender Version

Auditions and other extroverted activities often leave people feeling giddy. Maintain that great mood and sense of joint adventure by following up with an evening of dinner and dancing. There's nothing like a glitzy night on the town to make actors feel like the stars they ought to be.

SharpNote

This date is not ideal as a surprise activity, as many people have a mortal fear of the stage. Make sure your date agrees to this plan in advance. Unless you're a theater major or professional performer, you'll most likely be auditioning just for laughs, so encourage her not to take rejection too personally.

Required Gear

Unless the director has a specific piece in mind, you and your date will most likely be asked to perform a monologue from a play. Pick up something short and sweet at your local bookstore or library and practice with your date the night before your planned audition.

The Brown-bag Lunch Date

The Date

Enjoy a lunchtime concert—complete with brown-bag picnic and your date of choice.

Why It's Great

Does your date need a quick breather in the midst of a stressful workday? A lunch date may be the perfect solution, especially when combined with food and outdoor music. Many cities regularly hold lunchtime events weekly or monthly to help bring people downtown; check newspaper listings for a brown-bag concert or midday event near your date's office.

Big Spender Version

A traditional brown-bag lunch (i.e., sandwich, apple, carrot sticks, potato salad, cupcake) is just fine, but when you're really looking to spark romance, tote along a gourmet meal in a picnic basket. Not much of a cook? Don't worry. Simply head to the deli section of a high-end grocery store for beautifully prepared finger foods. Then pick a spot, spread out the picnic blanket, and dish out the food. If your date is able to take the afternoon off, make a day of it by lingering downtown and browsing art galleries and kitschy shops.

SharpNote

This date idea is especially pleasant in the spring, when it's not too hot—a perfect low-pressure first date or rendezvous with a longtime love. Also ideal for meeting online friends or blind dates, as your date will feel safe meeting in a public place, where you can showcase your gentlemanly nature.

Required Gear

Picnic food or brown-bag lunch, picnic blanket, napkins, plastic eating utensils, and lemonade or bottled water.

The Dog Day Date

The Date

Take out a dog—either yours or your date's. Enjoy a walk, hike, or picnic.

Why It's Great

Most people enjoy being in the company of animals. During a date, a dog becomes the ultimate wingman, providing fodder for hours of lighthearted conversation. Caring for an animal shows off your warmhearted sense of compassion as well as your responsible character.

Plan to walk to a nearby park for a picnic lunch. Consider bringing along dog toys such as balls or Frisbees to keep your canine "date" entertained. Don't forget a water bowl and treats.

No dog between the two of you? With volunteer dog walkers in demand, owning a dog is not required. Simply call your local Humane Society or SPCA. These organizations can sign you up as a volunteer dog walker, or at least point you in the right direction if you call ahead of time.

Big Spender Version

On your walk, swing by a pet store. Pick up a funny dog sweater or dramatic collar-and-leash set. Invite your date to help you dress the dog for a photo. True romantics will pick up a dog-themed picture frame for this photo—a great souvenir to commemorate a fun day.

SharpNote

A great first date. A must-do for dog owners.

Required Gear

Comfortable walking shoes, a water bottle and plastic bowl, and plastic bags for cleaning up a doggie mess.

The Go Fly a Kite Date

The Date

Take your date to the beach, a nearby hilltop, or other windy area for a picnic and some kite flying.

Why It's Great

Watching the movements of a flying kite can have a relaxing, trancelike effect on anyone used to the daily grind. Better still, focusing your date's attention on the kite can ease the pressure of finding a conversation topic. Finally, the whole idea of getting the flying machine airborne provides a sense of joint adventure and accomplishment.

If you're not a kiting professional, pick up a simple, inexpensive kite from a toy store. Hilltops are typically the best places for kite flying, since the terrain and pressure isobars create winds in various directions. Check your local paper for kite-flying festivals, such as the one on the National Mall in Washington, DC. These events are great places to learn more about kiting or to just sit back and watch.

Big Spender Version

Visit a hobby shop to learn more about kites and buy one you'd like to try out. Kites come in a variety of shapes, sizes, colors, flying styles, and price points. Some kites can be as pricey as fancy bicycles!

SharpNote

Advise your date to wear comfortable clothing and shoes.

Required Gear

A kite, plenty of string, a windy location, your jacket, athletic shoes for the climbing, and a pocket knife for cutting down your kite.

The Con-cher-to Date

The Date

Impress your date with your musical talents.

Why It's Great

Ever wonder why musicians get all the women? It's the music. Even if you're not especially musically inclined, if you've ever learned to play an instrument, your date will appreciate your effort to compose a musical piece especially for her. Brush up on the music that you know how to play, then choose a solitary location with good acoustics. Don't worry if you don't have the technical skill of Wolfgang Amadeus Mozart or Stevie Ray Vaughan—the fact that you're making an attempt should be enough to put a smile on your date's face.

It's a good idea to have another instrument handy just in case your date feels the urge to join in. Provide simple instruments such as egg shakers or a conga drum to avoid complications. Plan a picnic dinner or lunch before your "concert."

Big Spender Version

Spring for an accompaniment! Many music schools help their students book "gigs"—even private performances for two. Consider the instruments that will complement your playing and song stylings. Bring along some wine, candles, and anything that will help set the mood (and deflect from your less-than-professional performance).

SharpNote

If your performance goes extremely poorly, be sure to find humor in the situation and laugh at yourself—after all, who has time for a big-label record deal, anyway?

Required Gear

Instruments, picnic fare, and bottled water.

The Speak-er Up Date

The Date

Treat your date to an afternoon (or evening) listening to an educational speaker. Follow up with a meal that matches the speech's theme.

Why It's Great

Listening to a speaker can expand your knowledge base and lead to some interesting and easy-flowing date conversation. Plus, lectures are often free. Find a lecture that interests you and your date by checking your local paper's arts section or going online to consult the events calendar of your town's university, cultural center, bookstores, or churches.

Follow up with a walk to a coffeehouse to discuss the merits of the speaker's presentation.

Big Spender Version

Big-name speaking engagements often charge an entrance fee. If the speaker is selling a book or other product, take a chance and buy the material. Whatever the speaker's topic, continue on the theme. If your speaker is a horticulturist—a specialist on orchids, for example—follow up the lecture by visiting a greenhouse and purchasing a special flower and plant food as a date souvenir. Similarly, if you and your date just sat through a lecture on Italian history, continue the evening at an Italian restaurant for a great meal of pasta and Italian wine.

SharpNote

Do some intelligence gathering on your date's interests prior to choosing a topic that sounds like it might be interesting. No date wants to sit through several hours of droning on about a subject that doesn't interest her.

Required Gear

Tickets, notepad, and pencil.

The Not Just a Movie Date

The Date

Use your camcorder or MPEG-enabled digital camera or even your mobile phone to make your own short film, sketch-comedy skit, or music video.

Why It's Great

People love being in front of the camera. When this date ends, you and your date will come away with some home-movie material and a few laughs. You can either plan your shots or just start recording impromptu lines and gestures.

Breaking the ice is key in this date. If your date starts off camera shy, position yourself as a mediocre or goofy actor that she will easily be able to outperform. Give your date top billing!

Big Spender Version

If you have access to a computer, you can splice together sounds and effects to create a professional-looking final product. Alternatively, turn your raw footage over to a film student at your local university. For a fee, the film department will *really* make you and your date's work look good. Burn your movie onto a CD or DVD for a date souvenir.

SharpNote

Great for first dates or dates with women who will bring their kids.

Required Gear

Camcorder, video-enabled digital camera or mobile phone, an extra battery, and any props you choose.

The Climbing Date

The Date

Check out natural rock formations or your local climbing gym to experience rock climbing or bouldering.

Why It's Great

Climbing is a team-building activity, complete with a bit of exercise and the reward of a spectacular view or awesome sense of accomplishment at the end. And because so many athletic gyms now feature climbing walls, this date does not necessarily require a nearby mountain peak. These gyms or outdoors shops can also rent you any climbing gear you may need. Add a small bag of energy bars, rock candy, and red licorice ropes to create a memorable experience.

If you're both beginners, try a climbing gym before hitting the real thing. The staff trainers can give you the rundown on rock-climbing jargon, harnesses, equipment, and climbing techniques.

Big Spender Version

Want to start off kicking? Contact one of the climbing trainers at your local gym or outdoor-gear shop for a private lesson for you and your date. Arrange for a picnic at your summit point, or as far as you make it on your first try! For a *really* over-the-top date, consider traveling to a famous climbing spot and hiring a trainer at this location.

SharpNote

"Bouldering," or short-distance, minimal-height rock climbing, is an option that doesn't require a harness and ropes. Great for a first date with an athletic woman.

Required Gear

Ropes, harnesses, carabiners, climbing shoes, and—most important—professional training and climbing safety instruction, all available at your local outdoors store.

The Game Show Date

The Date

Take your date out to watch a favorite game show—as a member of the studio audience. Or create a game show–themed outing in your hometown by arranging a "game show day."

Why It's Great

Movies and concerts can be contrived date experiences, but a game show is a fun and interactive form of entertainment for those lucky enough to be in the audience. Getting tickets to the show requires only some research and persistence. Visit www.tvtix.com or www.studioaudiences.com for information.

If you prefer the at-home version of this date, give the game a genuine feel by providing prizes and parting gifts. Don't forget snacks for your contestants and the studio audience: pretzels, chips, and other finger foods work best.

Big Spender Version

If you are hell-bent on getting into the studio audience of your favorite game show, try the regular avenues of obtaining tickets, and then go local. Most game shows are taped in Los Angeles and only come to other cities for a week or two every few seasons, so consider taking a trip with your date. If you cannot arrange for tickets ahead of time, visit the studio lot where the game show is taped, as tickets are often given away at the studio gate on the morning of the show.

SharpNote

Whether playing at home or watching a taping, try to avoid being a game-show smarty-pants. Let your date get a few of the answers.

Required Gear

Somewhat stylish clothes and a bubbly personality can help you and your date charm your way into a game-show audience.

The Round the World Photo Date

The Date

Invite your date to take digital photos and computer-edit them to create one-of-a-kind postcards.

Why It's Great

Are there any places in the world that you wish you could visit? With the help of photo-editing software, it's possible to fake an entire vacation. Begin by opening an atlas or surfing the Internet to choose photos of the cities you and your date feel most drawn to. Once you have found your perfect "memories," save these images on a disk and head down to your local big-drugstore chain, many of which have digital-photo machines that allow you to combine images of you and your date and a famous background. Upload, combine, and voilà! You've got your postcards!

Big Spender Version

If you're a Big Spender with your own digital photo equipment, use a digital camera to take snapshots of you and your date. Upload these photos and use editing software such as Photoshop to drop the image of you and your date into pictures of all of your dream cities downloaded from the Internet.

SharpNote

Got your photos ready? Print and send or e-mail the photos to friends and family with "Wish you were here!" messages. Alternatively, purchase a matching set of photo albums prior to your date and paste in your shots—a great souvenir of your romantic "vacation."

Required Gear

Digital camera, scanner, printer or access to drugstore digital-photo machines, and a computer with an Internet connection.

The "Come Fly With Me" Date

The Date

Take your date, two lawn chairs, and a picnic lunch to the grassy area near a local airport for a relaxing meal that allows you to watch planes.

Why It's Great

Planes are fascinating—the way they take off suddenly, land gracefully, or—as in the case of small aircraft—sway back and forth before finally landing. A day spent watching the comings and goings of planes can be relaxing, conducive to conversation, and practically free. Best yet, this date requires minimal planning. You and your date will never run out of topics to talk about—from flight horror stories to trips you want to take.

Leverage the airplane theme to create a memorable experience. Pack your picnic on trays and serve peanuts or pretzels as a snack. Fill a cooler with a variety of sodas and find small, clear plastic cups to serve them in.

Big Spender Version

With some wine, minibottles of liquor, and a portable DVD player, you can treat your date to a "First Class" experience. Use a CD burner to put together the perfect soundtrack for your date. "Come Fly With Me" (Frank Sinatra), "Fly Like an Eagle" (Steve Miller Band), "I'm Flying" (*Peter Pan* soundtrack), and others will help you set the mood.

If you and your date need more stimulation, consider packing a pair of binoculars. Visit the check-in desks of the various commercial airlines that fly out of your airport and pick up a flight schedule booklet from each airline. (Flight schedules are also available on the Internet at respective airline Web sites.)

Once perched back at your viewing station, use your booklets and binoculars to identify where each plane is flying to or returning from.

SharpNote

If serving as your date's flight attendant doesn't sound like much fun, consider getting professional help. Many airports feature restaurants with flight-themed fare and large viewing windows. Call your local airport's hospitality staff or consult the Internet to find an eatery with the best view. Airport floor plans and restaurants are also available on the Internet.

Required Gear

Picnic blanket or lawn chairs, wine and corkscrew, themed food and drinks, picnic items, and ice.

The Feathered Friend Date

The Date

Treat your date to a bird-watching excursion. Add a picnic lunch or dinner.

Why It's Great

Bird-watching is a great way to get outdoors and into nature. Think of it as a softer version of hunting—you quietly stalk your prey until close enough to observe—but there's no pulling of a trigger or release of an arrow. Your date will be amazed at your tracking ability, coupled with your benevolent compassion for flying creatures great and small.

If you've never watched birds as a sport, scan the Internet for bird-watching sites such as www.birdwatching.com for pointers on how to take up the hobby. Also visit www.birders.com, a site that features a list of the top 100 North American birding sites. If you come up empty-handed with finding birds, try your local duck pond—where you can see and feed the birds.

Throw in a picnic to round out the experience.

Big Spender Version

If you'd like to spend money, you'll have no problem doing so with an activity like bird-watching. Bird-watching equipment abounds and goes far beyond a high-quality pair of binoculars. Look for bird callers, rangefinders, tripods, and mounts. Visit your local outdoor-gear store or bird-watching sites on the Internet.

SharpNote

Keep birdseed handy when birds are scarce, if feeding is permitted. The season and weather conditions may affect the quality of bird-watching. Note that this date is less conducive to conversation, as talking will scare away the birds!

Required Gear

Clothing you don't mind getting dirty, as well as hats, mosquito repellent, sunglasses, and comfortable, rugged shoes for marshy soil.

The Scrapbooking Date

The Date

Learn more about your date by asking her to bring a small box of mementos. Buy a scrapbooking kit and invite your date to put the pieces of your lives in order—together.

Why It's Great

This date creates the perfect setting for learning more about each other, and most of the requirements are already in your possession. If it's early in the relationship, it's best to create two separate scrapbooks and talk about the contents. For longer-term couples, one scrapbook of your relationship will document your romance—the way you went from two to one. Set up your scrapbooking materials on a large surface and keep finger foods available. Then open a bottle of wine to toast your creation! Scrapbooking kits retail for around $20.

Big Spender Version

For the ultimate scrapbooking experience, head to a craft store to choose your kit, but also purchase tissue paper, markers, glitter pens, ribbon—anything that would add a personal touch to the scrapbook. Since you'll be in the mood for reminiscing, find a restaurant that is special to your date, dine there when your scrapbooking is complete, and add a trinket from the dinner, such as a napkin or matchbook, to your date's scrapbook.

SharpNote

This date is better suited to a second or third date, as it may be too intimate for a first date.

Required Gear

Check out your local stationery shop, craft store, or department store for a scrapbooking kit. You and your date will supply the contents.

The Baking Date

The Date

Invite your date to bake together from scratch—cookies, pies, whatever. No boxed mixes allowed.

Why It's Great

In our hectic lives, baking often takes a backseat to other duties. Why not whisk your date back to the days of homemade cookies, cakes, pies, and beyond? Even if your baked goods don't turn out exactly as planned, you'll have a lot of fun making them! Stock up on aprons, ingredients, baking gear, and recipes before your date. It's even better if you have an intended purpose for your efforts—maybe a church bake sale? To add some creative flair, pick up sprinkles, colored sugars, and frosting tubes to add flowers or decorations to your sweets.

For maximum bonus points, consider baking a double batch and donating your baked goods to a local soup kitchen or retirement home. Call ahead to ensure your local facility accepts home-baked donations.

Big Spender Version

To truly impress your date from start to finish, try these tips: Present her with a gift—a personalized apron—before you begin. Then, after you've finished baking, present your date with a home-cooked meal that you prepared the night before and slipped into the oven while she was out of the room. She will be touched by your extra effort.

SharpNote

This is a great date for women who will bring their children. Some women may not feel comfortable going to your home for a first date.

Required Gear

Make a trip to the grocery store before you get cooking, and be sure you have enough bakeware.

The Five Fingered Date

The Date

Finger paint portraits of each other. Buy cardboard frames and have a hanging ceremony. Add pizza "portraits" for lunch.

Why It's Great

Ever wish you were a kid again? Not all of us can paint like Picasso, but everyone can find inspiration in finger painting. Finger painting portraits of each other is a fun, inexpensive, and easy way to remember your first date with someone special. To set up, arrange newspaper across your floor or on a table, arrange paints, and get to work! Keep paper towels handy for spills. Offer your date an old sweatshirt or apron to protect her clothing. When the portraits are ready, arrange them in cardboard frames and hang them on the wall. To top off your day of creativity, pick up pizza fixings and create portraits of each other on pizza crusts.

Big Spender Version

Arrange for you and your date to attend a one-time art class before painting your portraits. Supply blank painting pads and see if your newly acquired skills will translate to paper. Follow up your art lesson with a meal at her favorite restaurant.

SharpNote

A terrific first date, but note that some women may not be comfortable going to your home if they don't know you very well. Also great for women with children, especially if you include them in the painting!

Required Gear

Visit an art supply store for finger-painting kits and frames. Don't forget towels and soap for the post-paint cleanup.

The Biker Date

The Date

Rent a bike built for two and explore your town. Plan a route that ends at a nice restaurant, or pack a picnic lunch.

Why It's Great

You can plan your route so that you ride by locations—restaurants, schools, and childhood homes—that are personal and will spark conversation. Pack a backpack with plenty of cool drinks and energy bars. At the end of your journey, surprise your date with a picnic lunch.

Big Spender Version

Cycling can be tough on the, um, caboose. But special cycling pants can make your ride (and day after!) more enjoyable. Invite your date to meet you at a cycling-gear shop, and treat her to a great pair of padded cycling shorts, gloves, and a helmet. Suggest that she pack a change of clothes. Plan a route that concludes at a favorite restaurant. The two of you can make a quick clothing change and enjoy a meal. To avoid riding home on a full stomach, have your car waiting at the restaurant and arrange for the bike to be picked up later. Your date will take notice of your extra effort.

SharpNote

A terrific first date.

Required Gear

Check sporting-goods stores for bike rentals and equipment. For a picnic lunch, plan light foods that won't weigh you down for the ride home.

The Scavenger Hunt Date

The Date

Challenge your companion to a scavenger hunt that leads to the main event of the date.

Why It's Great

A scavenger hunt can provide fun for an hour or a full day, depending on how you design it. Any way you plan it, it builds to a satisfying climax and a well-deserved rest from the "hunt."

Pick a theme for your scavenger hunt that gives clues about the ultimate place where your date will end up. For example, answering clues that revolve around French history might eventually lead to a French bistro where coffee and a croissant are the reward. If your questions involve an art theme, your destination might be a museum. Be creative with your clues and final destination.

Send your date a letter or e-mail with her first clue. Your clue should lead her to the location where her next clue can be found. Follow with another two to ten riddles that lead her to your ultimate destination. You may choose to send your date a-hunting on her own and wait for her to arrive, but it's more fun if you join her.

Big Spender Version

If you're in a position to spend more time and money, hide a themed gift at every stopping point on the scavenger-hunt route. For example, on the museum hunt, present your date with small items from the museum gift shop. Your final gift should be the pin that admits her to the exhibit. Worried about leaving gifts out in the open? Carry these prizes in a backpack and hand one to your date after each clue is solved.

SharpNote

This is a fun first date or a great way to put the spark back into a longtime love. If your treasure hunt requires your date to do some walking, advise her to wear comfortable shoes.

Required Gear

Small note cards for writing out the clues, comfortable shoes, and a camera for documenting your adventure.

The Quiz Show Date

The Date

Quiz each other over coffee or drinks with twenty questions.

Why It's Great

There's no more direct way to learn about your date than by asking twenty questions. Keep the coffee or drinks flowing, and offer to field the first question. You can set the level of intimacy by the way you answer your questions. For a first date, you're looking to learn basic facts about your date, not to uncover her most private thoughts. For longer-term couples, this date idea is a great way to learn more about his or her feelings for you or to catch up on each other's hectic life. No matter how long you've been together, there's always more to learn.

Big Spender Version

For a more upscale date, move out of the coffee shop and into a nice restaurant that offers a multicourse tasting menu, such as those featured in French restaurants. Offer to answer a question or two with every course and a bonus question for each glass of wine.

SharpNote

Equally suited to first dates and long-term relationships.

Required Gear

Inquisitive minds!

The Changing Places Date

The Date

It's time to score points! Offer to help your date move her furniture.

Why It's Great

It's always fun to reinvent a space—and even more so with an extra pair of hands to help. First, take a Polaroid or digital photo of the room you'd like to rearrange, then move all the furniture out and remove everything from the walls. This is a great way to finally rid a room of clutter and piles of papers that seem to grow in nearly every living space. Sketch out some possible ways to rearrange the room. For added help, pick up some interior-design books, perhaps on feng shui. If it's a small space, try to rearrange the furnishings to make the room appear bigger. Once you're finished, take an "after" shot of the room, put both photos in a side-by-side frame, and hang it in the new space. Follow with a hearty meal as a reward for the heavy lifting.

Big Spender Version

Redecorate the room. Could the walls use a new coat of paint? How about new curtains for the windows? Help your date pick out new items and do the work. As a surprise, gift her with a new piece for the room—a coffee-table book or piece of art, for example. That way, the room will always have a piece of you in it.

SharpNote

Better for a third date and beyond.

Required Gear

For rearranging, wear comfortable clothes. For redecoration, bring old clothes and the tools you require.

The Corny Date

The Date

Kick off the season of harvest moons and autumn breezes by driving out of town and getting lost—in a cornfield maze (or rather, *maize*).

Why It's Great

Talk about an original date. Since 1986, cornfield mazes have been sprouting up all across the country. Typically open from September to November (depending on the climate), these cornstalk labyrinths make for an interesting and enlightening date. Want to know how your date responds under pressure or frustration? You'll glean crystal-clear insight into her personality after two hours of running into dead ends and walking in circles.

The best part of this date? There's a designated beginning and ending. If it goes well and you discover you make a great, cohesive team of maze sleuths, then make plans to stop at a local coffee shop on your way back, to warm up and laugh about your adventure. If not, you're off the hook, and are free to go your separate ways.

Add a romantic twist by packing a picnic and going to the maze on a weekday afternoon—there are usually fewer crowds during the day, and there's nothing like a cool, crisp autumn lunch out in the country.

To find a maze near you, visit www.cornfieldmaze.com and click on your state. Admission prices are around $10 per person.

Big Spender Version

No cornfield maze near you? Plan a trip to the nearest one and make a weekend out of it. Continue the country theme by staying at a bed and breakfast outside the city limits, and then skip the interstates and take the back roads to your destination.

SharpNote

Cornfield mazes are independently operated, so if you're planning to bring along a picnic, it's a good idea to call and confirm that bringing in food is appropriate. If you do have a maze near your city, this is a great first-date activity—it even works well as a group date.

Required Gear

Comfortable clothing and shoes are a must. Nighttime maze-goers require flashlights, jackets, and (in some areas), bug repellent.

The Rain Forest Date

The Date

Take an afternoon stroll in a tropical rain forest by exploring your local botanical garden. Afterward, visit a nursery and create your own jungle.

Why It's Great

There's something magical about escaping the hustle and bustle of the city to slip away to a lush forest complete with hazy waterfalls, overgrown trees, and fish-filled streams.

Check out your city's Convention and Visitors Bureau Web site to find the nearest botanical garden. Then invite your date on an adventure that will take her worlds away, as you meander past cocoa trees from South America, mahogany trees from Brazil, and jacaranda trees from Mexico's countryside. You can spend hours in the gardens or greenhouse, or quickly escape for a lunch break.

After discovering the flora of other lands, visit a local nursery and plan your personal botanical garden. On a budget? Decide which plants you'd like to have and then order their seeds online—simply type in the name of the plant plus the word "seeds" and you'll find a plethora of resources.

Big Spender Version

Follow up your rain-forest date with a trip to an exotic restaurant. Keeping with the theme of faraway lands, choose a Brazilian café or other South American restaurant.

Additionally, increase the number of tropical plants that you can grow by buying your sweetie a portable greenhouse. This way it won't matter if you live in New York City or Key West, Florida.

SharpNote

This is a fun first date, conducive to easy conversation.

Required Gear

No gear required for phase one of the date, botanical garden. Phase two, creating your own garden, will require some equipment, should you have a large area to work with, or simply a few pots and soil for a small balcony or terrace.

The Top Gun Date

The Date

Set your sights high by inviting your date to a local air show.

Why It's Great

Typically free, local air shows are easy on the pocketbook and offer larger-than-life high-flying action. This is a great first date for those who are still mastering the art of conversation, as there's hardly any time for a meaningful chat between low-flying acrobatic airplanes.

Pack a cooler with munchies, take a blanket, and enjoy the afternoon. Afterward, stop by the video store and rent *Top Gun* to continue fueling your high.

Air shows are usually organized in the spring or summer. Check with your local Convention and Visitors Bureau to find the date, time, and location.

Big Spender Version

Follow the air show with dinner at the highest restaurant in town, where you can catch an eagle-eye view of the city while you muse about your day.

Alternatively, take your meal into the air. Arrange for dinner service aboard a private flight for your own tour of the sky.

SharpNote

Great for first dates and double dates.

Required Gear

Comfortable clothes, blanket or foldable chairs, drinks, and snacks.

The Urban Legend Date

The Date

Spend an afternoon or evening exploring the locations where local legends occurred!

Why It's Great

There's just something about investigating local legends that really gets the adrenaline pumping. Remember the story of the hook-armed man terrifying a teenage couple at Make-out Point? Or the one about the old woman who passed away but still roams her home at night? Why not verify these stories for yourself? Or at least visit the locations—just for fun!

Gather several couples together for your exploration. The more people the better, as each participant has probably heard a different version or may know other legends that you've never heard of.

Even if you're a native, you'll find that this idea requires some research prior to your date. Some of the best information on local lore may come from friends, family, older neighbors, or coworkers. Libraries and the Internet are also good sources.

Big Spender Version

Turn your urban-legends outing into a theme date by dining at a legendary locally owned restaurant. Extend your date by signing up for a walking tour of your city. Contact your town's Convention and Visitors Bureau for information.

SharpNote

Great for first dates and group dates. If you're planning a first date, make it just the two of you.

Required Gear

A map, a flashlight, and an intrepid spirit.

The Arcade Date

The Date

Remember when you didn't have a driver's license and had to beg Mom to drop you off at the mall to meet your date for an evening of window-shopping and arcade playing? Relive the forgotten fun of your preteen years with the Arcade Date, but with a few changes.

Why It's Great

Not only do you now have a driver's license, but you also probably have your own car; things are already looking better for you this time around.

Set yourself and your date up with a pocketful of change, and have a ball challenging each other to two-player games of Frogger, Pac-Man, and Donkey Kong. Race each other down city streets, over waterfalls, and through tunnels as you play games that you haven't touched since Atari was a household name.

Follow your action-packed night by indulging in long-forgotten arcade delicacies such as drippy, sloppy nachos topped with jalapeños, big fat hot dogs glistening with juice, and an extra large Coca-Cola.

Be sure to play one of those games where you can win your date a prize—there's nothing like a stuffed yellow dog to make her reflect on your date and smile.

Big Spender Version

It won't be long before you remember why you don't eat like that anymore. Consequently, burn off those extra thousand calories by leaving the arcade and venturing to your local amusement park—and with amusement park prices as high as they are these days, you'll see why this is the Big Spender version of this date! Ride the roller coaster, go head-to-head on the bumper cars, and cool off on the log ride...and you might as well end the evening right: by sharing a fuzzy helping of cotton candy. Just remember to revert back to your health kick in the morning....

Don't want to fall off your diet wagon? Treat your date to a home video game system of her own. Then settle in a for a night of competitive hardball!

SharpNote

Great for first dates and dates with women who have children, especially if you invite them along!

Required Gear

Comfortable clothing, shoes, and lots and lots of quarters.

The American Dream Date

The Date

Walk through high-end model homes or any big homes for sale in your area. Add lunch or dinner to make it complete.

Why It's Great

There's something exciting about imagining what your dream home would look like. Turn this excitement into a date by inviting your honey to join you in visiting high-end model homes or large homes for sale. Pick up some brochures beforehand so your date can choose the houses she'd like to see. The driving time and homes you see should give you plenty to talk about.

Big Spender Version

Charitable organizations and local decorators often host a "Parade of Homes" or a "Design House" as a fund-raising event. Check out the home design, real estate, or calendar sections of your local newspaper to learn when these events are scheduled and how to purchase your tickets.

In a typical home parade, you and your date will have a chance to see twelve homes or a large home with six to eight rooms designed by various local designers. Many feature lavish entertainment areas, luxurious pools, and outdoor fireplaces. Treat your date to dinner in the neighborhood where the home you view is located.

SharpNote

A fun first date.

Required Gear

Good walking shoes, brochures, and a "homing" instinct.

The Going to the Races Date

The Date

Visit a horse racetrack and treat your date to a day of betting on the ponies.

Why It's Great

Remember when Eliza Doolittle went to the races in *My Fair Lady*? How about Julia Roberts in *Pretty Woman*? If not, all you need to know is that among the highlights of these chick flicks were women dressed to the nines, watching the steeds through their opera glasses. Why not bring this magic movie moment to life for your date? Unless the race you choose is at one of the more traditional North American venues, there aren't likely to be scores of women in fancy hats, but you and your date can certainly enjoy the same exhilaration. Encourage your date to bet on the horse she favors; consider choosing your horse based on the name she likes most rather than by the odds, to make your bet less serious and your victory more personal.

For extra fun, rent *My Fair Lady*, *Pretty Woman*, or *Seabiscuit* prior to your outing.

Big Spender Version

Buy tickets to a big race and treat your date to the VIP section, where food and drink may be served. You'll enjoy the best view. After the race, spring for a meal at the clubhouse.

SharpNote

Not all women will be interested in horse racing or gambling, and some may even find such activities offensive. Determine this preference prior to planning this date.

Required Gear

Tickets, hats, binoculars, and sunglasses.

The Builders' Date

The Date

Put together a complicated puzzle or build a Lego mansion. Follow up with a trip to a buffet restaurant where you can "build" your own meal.

Why It's Great

Legos aren't just for kids anymore. Load your CD changer with CDs, take out some chips and beverages, and begin building. This fun date works equally well with blocks or a puzzle. As you work together, keep the conversation lively with game-related stories from childhood. Once you've finished your masterpiece, head out to an all-you-can-eat buffet where you can assemble your own meals.

Big Spender Version

If Legos, building blocks, and puzzles aren't challenging enough, try something a bit more technical: building and launching a model rocket. Model rocket sets can be purchased at most hobby and some toy stores. It's a great way to challenge your and your date's technical abilities, and then watch your creation take off into the air.

SharpNote

Great for first dates or taking out women and their children.

Required Gear

Building game, snacks and drinks, comfortable clothing, and a work surface, such as a dining table or open floor space.

Chapter Four

Great Dates

Special Seasonal Dates

The Waterfront Date

The Date

Spend a day relaxing on the water. Add a picnic lunch.

Why It's Great

There's just something about being out on the water that feels *perfect* to most people. In addition to being a great date for Fourth of July weekend, you can apply this summertime goodwill to a date scheduled for any other time of year. These days, even the driest of desert cities is home to a few reservoirs or man-made bodies of water. More often than not, canoes, paddleboats, and other watercraft are available for rent at the shore or close by. Pack a yummy picnic lunch and take your date out for a leisurely float. You'll find plenty to talk about—or not—as you prefer. Looking to spend a whole day on the water? Bring along a deck of cards and a small battery-operated radio.

Big Spender Version

As long as you've gone to the trouble of packing up all your gear and driving to the lake, you might as well stay for a spell. Many of the large, recreational lakes have houseboats and sailing or fishing boats for rent. This way you can extend the magic and live on the water for a couple of days. Don't forget to pack great reading material and a chess set or backgammon board. You and your date will enjoy plenty of sun-dappled, romantic hours.

SharpNote

While you're on the water, try your hand at some lake or river fishing, as local regulations allow. Note that fishing may not be appropriate for dates with women who find it cruel.

Required Gear

Boat shoes, life vests, sun hats, and sunscreen are advised. Depending on the time of year, jackets may be a good idea. Don't forget to pack a seaworthy picnic lunch and bring along music, games, and optional fishing gear.

The Great Pumpkin Date

The Date

Pick out and carve pumpkins. Then roast the seeds for a Halloween treat.

Why It's Great

Since costume parties aren't for everyone and trick-or-treating isn't an option for adults without kids in tow, this activity gives you and your date a great way to celebrate Halloween. Plus, it isn't limited to late October—fresh pumpkins hit the stands September through November, making this a great date idea throughout the fall season.

Pumpkin carving welcomes conversation and requires little skill—triangles and squares aren't too hard to cut. And pumpkin seeds are an easy and delicious treat—just roast them in the oven with a little salt.

Big Spender Version

Take a trip to a pumpkin farm to pick out your pumpkins. This may involve some time in the car, which will give you a chance to talk and get to know each other. Then splurge on a pumpkin-carving kit, complete with pumpkin face patterns to make your carving a little more artistic and challenging.

To find the freshest pumpkins, check your local newspaper for ads featuring pumpkin farms and ranch stands. You can also look up greenhouses in the Yellow Pages; they often grow pumpkins seasonally or know where you can go to pick your own.

SharpNote

Great for a first date and for dates with women who will bring their children. Note that some women may not feel comfortable spending time at your home on a first date.

Required Gear

Pumpkins, carving utensils, and an oven. Old clothing is advised.

The Haunted Date

The Date

Get into the spirit of the season by visiting a "haunted" house.

Why It's Great

Seasonal dates related to holidays are opportunities to score big points. After all, she chose to spend her Halloween with *you*, so you'd better make it good. No sweat: You've got a great date planned!

Take the opportunity to get traditional. There's something about engaging in traditional activities that makes a date seem more special and the date planner more charming. Find a haunted-house event in your area. Some are put together by private parties, while others are seasonal revenue-builders for local charities (more points for you, of course). Follow up with a great dinner.

Big Spender Version

Hire a professional special-effects makeup artist to make you and your date look as wild and gory as you wish. Some artists can even airbrush your entire body to match your face!

SharpNote

Most women prefer suspenseful haunted houses to outright gory ones. If you'd like to err on the side of sophistication, consider a "real" haunted house. Many cities offer historical haunted-house walking tours. Read up on the house prior to your date.

Required Gear

Most regions require warm clothing during October, particularly if the haunted house you choose requires you to stand in line outside. You might also consider giving your date a little gag gift as a memento; think vampire teeth or fake blood.

The Halloween Party for Two Date

The Date

Throw a spooky monster bash for two.

Why It's Great

Most people have fond memories of dressing up and going trick-or-treating on Halloween. Remember all those school carnivals? Haunted houses? Spooky movies? Why not an entertaining date?

Take your date back in time by carving a jack-o'-lantern together. Afterward, light a fire, turn off your porch light to dissuade trick-or-treaters, and take in a scary movie marathon of corny, old fright films such as the *Dawn of the Dead* series.

Big Spender Version

Go a step further by preparing a preparty meal. Keep it simple with easy-to-eat party food, including finger sandwiches, queso and chips, and—of course—some pumpkin pie. This is also a great opportunity to show off your bartending talents by making up your own witches' brew. Consider ours:

Witches' Brew Recipe

2 ounces Yellow Chartreuse
1½ ounces Blue Curaçao
½ ounce brandy, spiced
¼ teaspoon ground cloves
Dash nutmeg
Dash allspice

Shake all the ingredients together and serve in a chilled glass.

SharpNote

The scary-movie portion of this date works best if you and your date know each other well—perfect for scary-moment snuggling.

Required Gear

Movie rental, blanket for snuggling, pumpkin and jack-o'-lantern carving tools, food and drinks.

The Christmas Tree Date

The Date

Hit the road in search of a Christmas tree—for *her*. Chop it down and haul it back to her place.

Why It's Great

As with the Haunted Date (page 178), there's something about planning traditional seasonal activities that makes the date—and your efforts—feel more special. A year from now, she may not remember the dinner she had with the guy before you, but she'll always remember the Christmas she spent with you.

Make this time of year work to your advantage. Offer to help her pick out a Christmas tree the old-fashioned way. She'll no doubt be up for an adventure and will appreciate your exhibition of Paul Bunyan–like manliness (whether you're built like Paul Bunyan or not).

In November and December, it's common to see Christmas tree stands on every dirt lot in town. Skip those and make a date to go out of town to pick out and chop down your own.

Many nurseries have or are affiliated with tree farms and can direct you to a spot where you can cut your own Christmas tree. In addition to enjoying a scenic ride out of town, you and your date will have a chance to get out into the fresh air and pick a tree that will be that much fresher than those in town. Be sure to ask her to choose the tree. Complete your adventure with a hot lunch at a local café. Haul the tree back to her place and offer to help clean up the needles.

Has she already got a tree? Ask her to come along and help you choose yours. Pick the one she likes best.

Big Spender Version

Invest in the newest, trick, commemorative, limited-edition, special, wa-zoo ornament or tree topper of the season. Get one with the year on it and have it personalized. These commemorative ornaments are often made by companies like Christopher Radko, Waterford Crystal, Lenox, and Hallmark, and generally appreciate in value after they are no longer available.

SharpNote

A good first date, but a long one, so make sure you like her enough for the ride home. Realize that cutting down Christmas trees may not be attractive to environmentally inclined women or those who do not celebrate Christmas.

Required Gear

Warm clothing is a must. Consider packing a thermos of hot chocolate for the car. Some Christmas tree farms will provide you with the tools you need to cut down your tree, but call ahead to make sure. Otherwise, you'll need an ax or saw, a pair of work gloves, and a long line of sturdy rope to secure the tree to your car. If you've got a new car, consider packing an old blanket to protect your paint from the evergreen needles and sap.

Make sure there's a tree stand and ornaments waiting at home. Otherwise, pick up a stand and decorations on your way back.

The Gingerbread Date

The Date

Invite the object of your affections to your place for an afternoon or evening of gingerbread-house building. Follow up with a meal out and the delivery of your product to a local children's hospital or shelter.

Why It's Great

Women are impressed when men take the time to cook. Combine this with a little charity and you've got a winner.

Your date will either be dazzled by your baking and building skills or amused by your lack of them. Either way, she'll have a good time helping you build a gingerbread house—or for those who are less ambitious, helping you make and decorate holiday cookies. This activity is perfect for low-key conversation and will definitely be memorable.

Because building a gingerbread house is a big job, consider obtaining a pattern or kit and starting before your date arrives. You'll need to prepare the gingerbread walls and let them cool before beginning your assembly and decoration. Look for gingerbread kits available in many cooking and craft stores. You can even "cheat" by purchasing the gingerbread walls at a local bakery.

Once your masterpiece is complete, head out for a bite and deliver the house to a local children's facility. You'll get extra points for being so civic minded. Call ahead to ensure that your chosen hospital or shelter is able to accept your donation.

Big Spender Version

Ready for volume? Donate a "gingerbread-house building day" to a local children's hospital or shelter. You'll have to contact the facility's director regarding your intended contribution and let the hospital or shelter make the arrangements for your gingerbread dough, then show up to help with your date.

SharpNote

While this idea will work for a first date, some women may be uncomfortable with spending time in the home of a guy they just met; save this one for Date Two and beyond.

Required Gear

Get your gingerbread house recipe and materials prior to the date. Purchase plenty of decorating supplies and a sturdy piece of cardboard covered in foil to serve as your base.

The Fa-la-la-la-la Date

The Date

Spend an evening caroling and lifting the spirits of others less fortunate than you (and we don't just mean those without your hottie date).

Why It's Great

Again, engaging in traditional seasonal activities is always a winner. Combine this with a showing of altruism, and you're all set.

This date should be about the singing, so consider making this date a group event. There will be less pressure on you (and your voice) and you can always pair off later for a mug of hot chocolate and a meal.

Studies show that the holiday season is a time when many people, particularly senior citizens, get depressed and appreciate additional company. Consider caroling in front of or inside a nursing home or hospital for maximum date points.

Big Spender Version

This date is perfect for renting a well-stocked limo for a group of friends—especially your date's friends! Make sure the limo has a sunroof for peering out. If you can find one equipped with a karaoke machine, do it. It will make the singing sound *sooo* much better. Have thermoses of hot chocolate, spiced tea, and other cold-weather goodies on hand.

SharpNote

Got a voice that sounds more like a dying cat than a sweet melody? Skip this date.

Required Gear

Warm clothing is generally required.

The "It's Beginning to Look a Lot Like Christmas" Date

The Date

Celebrate the romance of the yuletide season by taking a tour of decorated homes, town halls, or riverfront. Or go on a stroll through a lit park.

Why It's Great

It's hard to beat the romantic blend of holiday lights, Christmas music, a cold evening, and hot chocolate. This date will have the most hardhearted of Scrooges falling head over heels. If you plan to enjoy this activity by car, be sure to have a couple of holiday CDs ready, in addition to some hot chocolate for the toasty ride.

This activity also works well as an add-on to other dates, especially if you've just done the traditional dinner and a movie and want the evening to last just a little longer.

Big Spender Version

Go all out by splurging for a carriage, sleigh ride, or snowmobile. Follow your holiday trail of lights tour with dinner at a cozy restaurant, complete with a roaring fireplace, and then return to home for eggnog and a fire of your own.

Don't forget the mistletoe!

SharpNote

A great first date. Most cities turn on holiday lights the day after Thanksgiving and keep them lit until after the first of the year.

Before suggesting that the two of you stroll through the park, take a moment to check out your date's shoes. If she's donned her favorite Manolo Blahniks (i.e., high heels) then you may want to skip the mile-long walk and opt for the auto tour.

Required Gear

Blankets and an extra jacket, holiday CDs, and hot chocolate.

The Sit on Santa's Lap Date

The Date

Visit Santa and tell him if you've been bad or good; buy photos or treat your date to one of the items on her Christmas wish list.

Why It's Great

Not only does this date allow you to feel like a kid again, you'll also discover whether your date is willing to let her guard down. Best yet, you'll be treating her to an experience that savors the season—you can't sit on Santa's lap in the middle of August! Consider splurging on a photo of you and your date with Santa—a fun date souvenir.

Call your local shopping center for information on when Santa will be holding court for adults.

Big Spender Version

Why not enjoy Christmas a bit earlier by asking your date to help you choose one of the items from her Christmas wish list? After all, who doesn't enjoy the pampered feeling of picking out their own gift?

SharpNote

The modest version of this date is appropriate for first dates.

Required Gear

Holiday smiles.

The Snow Date

The Date

Have a snowball fight, go sledding down your favorite hill, and build a snowman.

Why It's Great

We've all seen those movie montages where couples play in the snow, making snow angels or having snowball fights. Looks fun, but how many of us actually get our there and make our own winter-wonderland romance moment? This date is your chance to bring the movies to life. Add some hot chocolate between activities, and your date is bound to be magical.

Big Spender Version

The best part of your date will most likely be the après snowball fight—when you head inside to warm up. Consider taking this date idea on the road to a ski resort; then warm up by the fire in the resort's lodge. After you are toasty and dry, treat your date to dinner in the lodge dining room. All that running around in the cold can really work up an appetite.

SharpNote

The two things that can cut this date short are cold fingers and colder toes. Encourage your date to dress warmly and bring along some extra socks and gloves—just in case. Then be romantic: Offer to switch gloves if her fingers get cold, since your gloves will already be nice and toasty. A great first date or activity for a date with a woman and her kids. You'll *really* warm her heart by inviting them along!

Required Gear

Warm, waterproof clothes. Objects to bring your snowman to life: carrots, scarf, buttons, etc.

The Cross-country Date

The Date

Spend a day walking in the woods—on skis.

Why It's Great

Most people love the idea of getting away for a ski trip, but generally, first dates and early dates are just too soon to spend that much time together (let alone deal with the sleeping-arrangement issue). In winter, late fall, or early spring, consider taking a day trip to an area with enough snow on the ground for cross-country skiing.

Cross-country skiing is easy; in fact, practically no actual skiing skills are required. And it's fun—putting on a pair of cross-country skis lets you glide through snow-covered wooded areas you'd otherwise sink into. Another plus: you can cross-country ski anywhere with enough snow; no pricey lift tickets required, and no ski-resort crowds.

Pack along some bottled water (it is exercise, after all) and a daypack with some hearty lunches and a thermos of hot chocolate. There's nothing better than a great sandwich in the middle of the woods on a cold day. You may also want to bring along some auto-heat bags to warm up your date's hands throughout the day.

Big Spender Version

There's almost nothing more romantic than a horse-drawn sleigh. Maybe it's the *clippety-clop* sound of the horse's hooves echoing in the night air, or you and your date snuggled together under a blanket, but dates just don't get any more romantic than this.

SharpNote

For those of you with a longtime companion, this date makes a great budget alternative to a pricey ski weekend.

Additionally, you can vary this date by using snowshoes instead of cross-country skis, but it's a bit more of a workout and may not be appropriate for a date who isn't athletically inclined. Skiing once the sun goes down is not advised.

Call local ski resorts to find out about cross-country trails in your area. It's always easier to maneuver on trails groomed for cross-country skiing. Otherwise, pick any snowy open area and get going!

Required Gear

Visit a local ski store for cross-country skis, shoes, and poles, or rent these at the park or trail office. Advise your date to wear several light (but warm) layers. Cross-country skiing can be a vigorous workout, and you'll be happy to have the opportunity to shed layers as you get warmer. We suggest a thermal underwear layer, a sweater, easy-movement bottoms (not jeans), and a windproof layer on top. Bring along a heavier parka for use when you're not skiing.

Appendix

The Great Dates

The Great Dates

The Great Dates

The Great Dates

Great Dates

By Category

First Dates

First Dates

First Dates

Second Dates and Beyond

Dates for Day *or* Evening

Dates for Day *or* Evening

Dates for Any Weather

Dates for Any Weather

Dates for Any Weather